ROBERT WARREN

Being Human, Being Church

Spirituality and mission
in the local church

Marshall Pickering
*An Imprint of HarperCollins*Publish

Marshall Pickering is an Imprint of
HarperCollins*Religious*
Part of HarperCollins*Publishers*
77-85 Fulham Palace Road, London W6 8JB

First published in Great Britain
in 1995 by Marshall Pickering

1 3 5 7 9 10 8 6 4 2

Copyright © 1995 Robert Warren

Robert Warren asserts the moral right to be
identified as the author of this work

A catalogue record for this book is
available from the British Library

ISBN 0 551 02905-6

Printed and bound in Great Britain by
HarperCollinsManufacturing Glasgow

Contents

Introduction

We live in days of remarkable change. The collapse of the Berlin Wall, and of the whole communist world on the far side of it, rivetted the attention of the whole world in recent years. As has the collapse of apartheid in South Africa and the green shoots of peace in Northern Ireland. Alongside, and part of, these great upheavals has been a striking outworking of the prophecy of the Magnificat about exalting the humble evidenced in the names of some present heads of state such as Lech Walesa, Vasclav Harvel and Nelson Mandela.

In the midst of such changes Christians, and the Christian church, have been functioning as leaven in the lump. Mother Teresa, Alexandr Solzhenitsyn, Archbishop Desmond Tutu, together with Archbishop Romero and countless unnamed martyrs, have not just born witness to faith in Christ, but been icons of a church functioning as leaven in the – often very unholy – lump.

Not that the upheavals we have witnessed have all been for the good. We have been, largely powerless, witnesses of the repeated tragedy of nations imploding in inter-tribal rivalry in the Lebanon, in Rwanda and in the former state of Yugoslavia, with devastating consequences – particularly for innocent civilian populations.

The West has escaped much of these destructive upheavals, though the Bosnian tragedy is an all too vivid reminder that there is no guaranteed immunity. Indeed, few can avoid the conviction that deep cancers eat away at the heart of what history may well come to describe the West as, 'a once great civilization'.

Certainly turmoil and uncertainty are all around. Questions abound. Is there more to life than an upturn in the economy? Is a growth economy for every country a sustainable way for humans to handle life on a planet of finite resources? What are the values that are to hold society together, now that Christendom is no longer the mortar of society? What are the long term effects of the breakdown of natural community and family?

Into this uncertain world the church is sent to participate in God's mission of love, through Christ, for the whole created order. A first order question is simply 'what sort of people ought we to be?' If the church is to participate in God's activity in these days of upheaval, how should we function? History makes it clear that the church has learned to fulfil many different roles according to its setting in history. As Aidan Kavanagh puts it

> That the Church begins to change in response to a changing world . . . can be affirmed in its shift from being an illicit religion prior to the fourth century . . . to being the religion of empire and culture in the fifth; in its shift from this to being tutor of civilization for teutonic and slavic barbarians after the sixth century and author of modern Europe and Western civilization as we have known it. This last period was that of Christendom, an arrangement based on the close correlation of Church and State in an earthly City of God.

He goes on to say of the present setting of the church

> The address of Church to world in the Christendom mold has been dissolving at least since the renaissance and seems to be reaching a terminal stage in our own days.[1]

It is into this situation that this book seeks to speak, in so far as the days in which we live raise questions about how the church should be the church. It is written in the conviction that the church of the West needs to learn, for the first time for over a millennium,

[1] Aidan Kavanagh, *The Shape of Baptism*, p. 154

how to be a missionary church – because we are now in a new missionary setting.

As such, this book is neither the first nor the last word on the subject. Rather I see myself as someone picking up a baton handed down by others, running with the ideas and practices, and keeping my eye on those to whom I am handing on such insights as I have gained so far.

This book is certainly not the first word on the subject. The concept and title of missionary congregations can be traced to the WCC report published in the 1960's, called *The Church for others*, subtitled *'the missionary structure of the church'*. Others have been working on this subject, not necessarily using the 'missionary congregation' terminology. A number of them are mentioned in the text. Certainly, I have been building on foundations laid by others.

In this endeavour I have appreciated the encouragement of the Board of Mission and its members, staff and various committees. They have not only given creative critique and constant encouragement but a helpful sounding board for ideas. However, I – not they – are responsible for the ideas in this book.

Nor is this book anything like the last word on the subject. Such a work must wait for another author, and maybe many years yet before a definitive work can be written. It is, rather, something like 'a starter for ten'. I am convinced that, in and beyond the second half of the decade of evangelism, the church needs to pay close attention to how it is the church. It is the single most important way to forward, in a healthy and sustainable way, the work of evangelism. To this end I offer this book as a contribution to the church's thinking and practice, well aware that I have spent more time exploring questions than defining answers in what follows.

My invitation to the wider church is to join me, and others, in picking up these ideas and running with them. Any author must expect criticism of what he writes. I am well prepared for that. However, what I hope will happen is that others will take up the central idea, of the church making a shift into mission mode, and do two things. I hope this book will provoke others to develop, refine and mature the thinking I offer. I also, and more importantly hope, that others will apply these ideas (mine, and others) at the local level so that a whole new generation of churches, rooted in contemporary culture, alive to God, and engaging with the work of renewing the whole creation to which the Spirit invites us, may emerge.

If this book can make a contribution to that goal, I for one will be well satisfied.

THE CHURCH IN
INHERITED MODE

1

The Church as the Primary Agent of Mission

The purpose of the church is to manifest an alternative way of seeing and living life.

John Westerhoff III,
Living the Faith Community, p.72.

It is time to take the church in for a service. 'Church' as we know it in the Western world has, after all, been 'on the road' for fifteen hundred years. During that time there has been little servicing, so it may well need an overhaul of substantial proportions. That may well not be easy since we are so used, perhaps especially in the Church of England, to a fixed idea of what the church is and should be. It is difficult to imagine anything different.

Our picture of the church usually begins with a romantic rural setting in which a beautiful medieval church, built on the highest piece of ground in the area is surrounded by a quaint mixture of attractive old housing placed seemingly at random, but usually below the level of the church. From the church emerges a clergyman (usually in our mental picture, an elderly one). Often more liked than understood, he is – after the building – what people mean by 'the church'. To this building, and with this man (or, now, woman), comes a motley group of people each Sunday morning. Fewer, if any, come now in the evening. It is all part of the fading glory of rural England.

In many ways our intuition serves us well. The church as we know it does have its roots in the rural community. The story of its adjustment to the large conurbations, is largely a story of 'too little, too late'. It is also a story of patterns of church life ill-adapted to urban life.

Such patterns of church life are, today, also ill-adapted to rural life either. The rural community is itself changing out of all recognition. It is no longer a close-knit community of people who have grown up all their lives in this one place, who know each other well, are intermarried, and live, work and belong within a narrowly defined geographical area. Rather it is a mosaic of subgroups and interlocking cultures. The 'locals' still exist, though often they are elderly. The younger generation have left in search of work or to go to university or college. They will not return. Even if they wanted to, they would find they could not afford the inflated house prices. Their place has been taken by the commuting executives who spend most of their lives far beyond any 'parish boundary', and by those in search of the 'good' or 'green life'. Ironically their very coming is one more nail in the coffin of that very rural idyll for which they long.

Slowly and quietly many transformations have been brought about in our English culture. Not least is the fact that today people relate 'sociologically' (with 'our sort of people') rather than geographically (with physically near neighbours). The cumulative effect on the traditional way of being church is that it fits with less and less of life as it is now lived.

This picture of the church in a typical rural setting may seem far from the experience of many people living in urban and suburban settings and worshipping in a large Victorian barn of a church. Yet that church is modelled on the rural church, for that is what the church took with it when, late in the day, it joined in the Industrial Revolution exodus from the country to the manufacturing centres of England. In both settings a further way of being church, typified by the Cathedral but stemming originally from the settled religious community of monastic orders, has played a formative part. The robed choir is just one of the ways of being church inherited from those monastic roots.

All of which alerts us to the fact that various influences have shaped the way the church is the church today. Moreover, it helps us to see that there have been different ways of being church down through the history of the church. We encounter the *church-in-the-home* in New Testament times as well as the soon-to-be-abandoned *Temple-church*.[1] Early church history introduces us to the *church-of-the-catacombs*. Here the church met underground in the vast burial places in Rome which eventually covered twenty kilometres of underground passages in which half a million Christians were buried.[2] Celtic Christianity gives tantalizing hints of *people-group churches*, much less settled and organized than the Roman parish system which replaced it, but nonetheless pointing to another way of being church.

There are two questions that such a brief excursion into church history raises for us today. First is the question as to whether we necessarily have the right model for the setting in which the church finds itself today. The whole of this book sets out to address that question. Second is the question of why such different models of being church have emerged. This introduces us to a fundamental characteristic of the Christian faith – namely its cultural adaptiveness.

The adapting faith

It is one of the striking features of the Christian faith that it has become so adaptive to different cultures to which it has spread. This may well go a long way to explain why it is arguably the most universal of the historic religions of the world. That ability to cope with new settings was there from the earliest days of the church. It was the issue which prompted the first ever Church Council meeting, the Council of Jerusalem. The church came together to seek to discern how to cope with an unexpected, and largely unintended, influx of Gentiles to the faith. The matter which needed to be decided on was 'on what terms do we let them in?' After debate, listening to stories of God's working among Gentile

[1] See Romans 16 for mention of house churches and Acts 2:46 for Temple worship.
[2] Desmond O'Grady, *Caesar, Christ and Constantine*, p.18.

people and weighing of the Scriptures, the Council came to the conclusion that minimum requirements were the order of the day. Gentiles could be Gentile-believers. They were not required to become Jews first, or as well.

For most other historic religions, the faith, and the culture in which the faith is founded, are both fixed in stone. Certainly to be an Orthodox Jew, or Muslim, there is a strong commitment to a particular cultural form. Church history shows, rather a double adaptive instinct in the Christian faith.

There has been continual adaptation of the faith to particular cultures. The message has been communicated in ways that different cultures could most readily engage with. We see Paul taking that approach in his sermon in Athens when, pointing to the altar 'to an unknown God', he declares: 'Now what you worship as something unknown I am going to proclaim to you'.[3] One writer has put this adaptation of the gospel to different settings in these terms:

> Just as Christianity became wedded to *logos* in Hellenism, and to authority and law in Romanism, it became wedded to nature and the natural world in all its various levels and regions in the Celtic world.[4]

Whilst not necessarily agreeing with his way of seeing how the gospel was communicated to a Roman culture, we can see the truth of what he says. We could well add that the key to communicating the faith in its original Jewish setting was the concept of *Messiah*. Such adaptation (or 'translation') of the faith poses questions for the church today as to how the faith can be communicated in our setting. We will consider this adaptation of the faith to different cultures when we ask what 'prophetic word' might encapsulate the Christian message in contemporary culture.[5] However, there is another form of adaptation which we should attend to here.

There has been continual adaptation of the way the church is the

---

[3] Acts 17:23.
[4] Noel Dermot O'Donoghue, *The Mountain Behind the Mountain*, p.15.
[5] See Chapters seven to nine.

church in different settings. The variety of ways of being church already noted goes deeper than the simple matter of where meetings are held. Deeper matters are involved. The various forms in which the church has expressed its life point to a commitment to operate in ways that can be described as 'culturally appropriate'. A classic example of this is the way that the church in England took shape as a feudal structure with the parson mirroring in the spiritual realm (and often not just there) the same role as the squire did in the social, employment and political life of rural England. It was a wonderfully appropriate model of being church *in that particular setting*. The downside is that we have inherited a way of being church that is essentially feudal. More often than not they are enlightened and godly forms, but that does not alter the fact that they are unlikely to work well in a culture which has changed beyond recognition. As Jose Comblin, the Brazilian theologian and activist amongst the poor, has put it:

> Most of us still live in the refuge of our parishes, which are more the relics of an antiquated Christianity than the first fruits of a new people won for Christ in the midst of today's world.[6]

The pressing need

A number of factors in our present situation make it imperative that the church addresses the question of how best to be the church today. The rapid and profound changes in culture alert us to the fact that the adaptive faith of the church needs to be finding new and more appropriate ways of expressing itself in our day.

The increasingly marginalized situation of the Christian Church should have a similar effect in provoking us to address this issue. Yes, there are stories of growing churches but they are not the norm. Yes, there are stories of great sacrifice and faithfulness among clergy and laity alike; but what if they are doing heroic

[6] Jose Comblin, *Being Human* p.26.

work with outmoded tools? Is it wise to row a losing battle against an ebb tide and offshore wind, when an outboard motor is to hand? Yes, the Church has some wonderful traditions inherited from the past, but they are well served by such resistance to change as is likely to increase the chances that those very traditions will die out with this generation of churchgoers?

If the Church is to be effective in communicating the faith in a Decade of Evangelism, it will need to address the issue of the Church itself. Indeed the Lambeth Conference of Bishops which met in 1988, and issued a call to a decade of evangelism, did so in the context of calling the Church's attention to the need to renew the face and life of the local church.

> This Conference calls for a shift to a dynamic missionary emphasis going beyond care and nurture to proclamation and service.[7]

In the pastoral letter which accompanied the Conference Report, it was stated:

> In many parts of the world, Anglicans have emphasized the pastoral model of ministry at the expense of mission. We believe that the Holy Spirit is now leading us to become a movement of Mission . . . The emergence of basic communities and house groups requires us to review our traditional structures in parishes and dioceses.[8]

The implications of these arguments are that the Decade of Evangelism is not simply about doing evangelism, important though that is. The Lambeth Conference clearly saw that the work of spreading the faith is intimately bound up with how the church functions. To do justice to such a Decade will involve taking the time, thought and opportunity to rework the fundamentals of what it means to be the Christian Church as we prepare for the twenty-first century.

[7] *Lambeth Conference 1988*, recommendation 44.
[8] *Lambeth Conference Pastoral Letter*, 7:23.

However, the motivation to look again at the way in which the Church expresses its life is not simply a matter of the need to adjust to major changes in culture, or to make the most of the Decade of Evangelism, or to respond to the call of Lambeth 88. The very nature of the Church itself requires that we pay attention to how it expresses the faith it seeks to proclaim.

The vital ingredient

Peter Ward, the Archbishop of Canterbury's adviser in youth work, tells of his puzzlement in his early days of being a Christian that 'Jesus did not preach the gospel'. He goes on to explain that he was somewhat unnerved by the fact that, having been raised in an evangelical faith, he was surprised to discover that 'the gospel' as a series of truth statements, was rarely on the lips of Jesus. Rather he approached everyone through the uniqueness of their particular situation. Zaccheus receives a request for hospitality, the Samaritan women a request for water. The woman taken in adultery receives the assurance that Jesus does not condemn her and the dying thief receives the assurance of being with Christ in paradise. Jesus addressed each person individually, not according to any set pattern.

It is equally possible to be rather puzzled by the lack of any strong emphasis on evangelism in the letters of Paul. Yes, to be sure, there are several calls to speak out our faith scattered through his letters, but it is hardly a major theme. What does dominate his teaching is the call to live holy lives in the community of faith. A good number of his letters have what are called 'household tables' which are lists of dos and don'ts covering home, family and work situations. However, each time they are preceded by a more detailed explanation of how Christians should live out their faith in harmony with one another. That theme, of being a community which lives the truth, is given priority in subject order and the lion's share of the teaching space. Typical is this excerpt from Colossians:

> Therefore, as God's chosen people, holy and dearly loved, clothe yourselves with compassion, kindness, humility, gentleness and patience. Bear with each other and forgive whatever grievances you may have against one another. Forgive as the Lord forgave you. And over all these virtues put on love which binds them all together in perfect unity.[9]

Why did Paul put so much emphasis on relationships within the church and comparatively little on 'preaching the gospel'. The reason is simply that Paul saw that *the primary way in which the gospel is preached is through the way that God's people share a common life shaped by the truth revealed in Christ*. As Lesslie Newbigin has put it, this is the key hermeneutic (meaning 'interpretation' or 'exposition/explanation') of the Good News:

> The only hermeneutic of the gospel, is a congregation of men and women who believe it and live by it.[10]

The point being made here is that it is the church which is the primary agent of mission. All too often this is overlooked. When it comes, for example, to thinking about evangelism, most Christians do not see the crucial and primary role of the church. We think more naturally of the work of *evangelists*, such as Billy Graham, or *evangelistic events* – whether old-style mission meetings or the newer forms of Seeker-services. Or again, not least as a result of the research of John Finney,[11] we think in terms of *friendship-evangelism* as the crucial means of bringing others to faith. More recently, from the work of the Catechumenate Network to that of Alpha Courses, the church's attention has been drawn to the importance of *evangelistic processes* rather than one-off encounters or events.

Yet all of these means are secondary to, and dependent on, the prior existence of the church. The church exists not simply as somewhere to which to take the person seeking after faith, but as

[9] Colossians 3:12-14.
[10] Lesslie Newbigin, *The Gospel in a Pluralist Society*, p.227.
[11] *Finding Faith Today*.

the supreme means by which God has established that the gospel should be demonstrated in human life and human community. That community is described in Scripture as nothing less than the Body of Christ. This means that how the church conducts its life is foundational to the whole work of proclaiming the good news of Christ. Which is why the subject is so important – not least in a decade in which the church is seeking to discover how to communicate the faith more effectively. The New Testament suggests that the answer is not simply 'tell it', but 'live it – together'. The work of evangelism does not in any way bypass the church. Rather it moves it to centre stage. This is good news indeed for the many people who faithfully serve and work in their local church. Doing this work well is the key to making Christ known. Our work is vital, which is why a thorough reconsideration of how we do it is so important.

The great opportunity

Despite the forces at work which seem to have marginalized the church, we stand today faced with a great new opportunity to speak the good news of Christ into our culture by the way we live that truth in the life of the local church.

The church is in a similar situation to British industry in recent years. It suffered from the fact that it was first into the Industrial Revolution, and therefore had to reshape a long history of, now outmoded, ways of opening. The church too seems often trapped by the sheer weight of its past. That has not always been so. The story of the spread of the faith to these islands, through Celtic and Roman missionaries alike, is a story of creative and fruitful ways of being church in a culture that was far from 'Christian'.

Because of its long history the church all too easily forgets its primary purpose. When that happens it seeks to maintain its own life as an end in itself, rather than an instrument in God's hands. As Jesus warned, saving our lives can often cause us to end up losing them. This unconscious 'preservation order' on how the church is the church can then result in the church marginalizing itself:

> For the majority of people in this country our churches are
> irrelevant, peripheral and seemingly only concerned with
> their own trivial pursuits.[11]

Yet there are hungers in our society that make the life of the
church, at least potentially, of great significance. Amongst those
factors are the following.

There is a great hunger for relationship today. Certainly the old
ways are breaking down. We see that not only in the increasing
breakdown of marriage but in the growing loss of any sense of
local community in vast swathes of our country. We can no longer
assume that a particular geographical area is in any necessary
sense a community. The breakdown of many social networks has
left people with a hunger for relationships, for some sense of
belonging. Christians understand this drive towards community
because they believe we are made in the image of a social God – the
Trinity. What the church needs to find today is ways of relating, of
establishing community, in a way appropriate to its setting. In
essence this will be much more on the basis of networks (fluid,
light-structured, democratic, motivational groups) rather than
traditional forms of operating.

> Our world is calling out for social structures that will be
> more fluid and flexible, more open-ended and mobile, more
> creative and adventuresome, less self-reliant and more inter-
> dependent in their basic orientation.[12]

There is also a great hunger for demonstration today. People want to
see whether it works. The church is called to be – the pilot project
of the new humanity established by Christ, an outpost of the
kingdom of God and the 'community of the Age to Come'.

Not least is the world looking for models of handling conflict.
This is the force which blows families, communities and nations
apart as has been seen so tragically in recent years, for example, in
Northern Ireland, the former state of Yugoslavia and in Rwanda.

---

[11] Robin Greenwood, *Reclaiming the Church*, p.156.
[12] Diarmuid O'Murchu, *Our World in Transition*, p.79.

The danger here is that the church handles conflict by sweeping it under the carpet, often because the feeling is abroad that 'Christians should not disagree'. A church where there was no conflict has little relevance to our society. A church that has found a way to handle conflict creatively will be good news to all around and in it.

The Council of Jerusalem (Acts 15), already referred to, gives us such a model. It is a community willing to listen to one another, taking time to weigh up issues. It is a community seeking to empower and help others, setting minimum boundaries only. It is a community which is willing to subsume personal convictions within the greater goal of seeking to discover God's will in any situation. I recall just such a situation in my previous church where an able group of leaders met to decide who should fill an important post in the church. Opinions varied greatly and a common mind seemed an impossibility. We stopped to pray, in silence, for five to ten minutes, seeking to submit our wills to God's will and discern his mind. The result, as we went round the room one by one, was that everyone identified their first choice as the same person.

Life did not, however, always work out so easily and wonderfully, either in that church, or indeed in the Council of Jerusalem. Acts 15 ends with Paul and Barnabas falling out with each other about whether to give Mark another chance or not. But the truth remains, that there is a longing to see relationships work, to see the truth of God's call to love being practised. Conflicts in the church can seem such a distraction from getting on with the real work; but *this is the real work*. When people come near such a community they will instinctively know how real the relationships are.

There is also a great hunger for meaning and a sense of belonging. The current breakdown of many social networks may well be due to the claustrophobic and controlling atmosphere in previous patterns of socializing. There is little likelihood of a return to such ways of working. However, 'doing your own thing', 'feeling free', and 'being independent' cut us off from others. Yes, from their controlling and dictating influence, but also from the affirmation and identity we gain from relationship with others. It is in and through relationships that we find ourselves.

For all these reasons, the church is placed with a strategic opportunity to proclaim the gospel in language that our society can understand. It is the language of love, of belonging and community. It will have to be free of any foreign accents of control, manipulation and pretence. But such a way of relating will be good news for a society that is both fragmented and searching for meaning and a sense of belonging. As John Westerhoff, a great Christian educationalist put it:

> The purpose of the church is to manifest an alternative way of seeing and living life.[13]

How that might come about is what this book is about.

Agreeing terms

Before we can go any further we need to define the words which are being used. A whole series of contrasting terms are used today to draw a distinction between how the church has operated and how it needs to operate in the future.

The first contrasting pair of words is contained in the phrase 'moving from maintenance to mission'. Here *maintenance* and *mission* are being contrasted. There is a hidden danger in this terminology, namely that plenty of 'maintenance' needs to go on and does go on in healthy 'mission-orientated' churches. So, for example, if mission is seen in terms of bringing an individual to faith, then the moment that happens we will need buildings in which that person can meet and worship with others, people employed to help support, nurture and equip such people, and organizational structures through which they can express their service of God. Certainly, it could well be that we could find simpler structures, but all such work is actually 'maintenance'.

The real distinction here is between maintenance seen as an end in itself – maintenance is our mission – and maintenance as a

[13] John Westerhoff III, *Living the Faith Community*, p.72.

means of forwarding mission – 'maintenance is for mission'. However, valid though this distinction is, it does imply an idealistic notion of mission which makes all 'maintenance' unnecessary. Having spent much of my parochial ministry seeking to develop structures which enabled, rather than inhibited, mission, I am reluctant to use this terminology.

The second pair of words are contained in the phrase 'the shift from pastoral to mission mode'. Here *pastoral* and *mission* are being contrasted. It is a contrast which the Lambeth Conference of Bishops in 1988 used. They drew a distinction between the church focused around 'care and nurture' and the church focused around 'proclamation and service'. The bishops spoke also about the 'pastoral model' of the church and the church as a 'movement for mission'.

The terms *pastoral* and *missionary* are useful if used to define two ways in which the church has operated *because of the surrounding culture*. The church has operated in *pastoral* mode because it has been set in a Christendom culture where the values of the community are shaped by the Christian faith and where the great majority of people (until relatively recently) have been baptized members of the church. In contrast, the church has functioned in *missionary* mode when the context for its life has been a culture that is not specifically Christian. During the Roman occupation, and in the time of Celtic missions, the church was operating in just such a setting. Today our culture is changing so profoundly that we are now moving out of such a pastoral or Christendom setting into a missionary one.

For these reasons it is attractive to use the words *pastoral* and *missionary*. However, there are dangers with those terms. The Lambeth Conference, aware of this, spoke of shifting from a purely pastoral mode to a pastoral-in-mission mode. That was done to express the obvious fact that being a missionary church does not mean abandoning pastoral care. Indeed, such care has been a major contribution to the church's mission.

However, there are several reasons why it seems best not to use these terms. First, once we introduce the subtle distinction of 'purely pastoral' to 'pastoral-in-mission' the terms become fuzzy, cumbersome and less clear. Second, the words 'pastoral' and 'missionary' are in danger of being overloaded with meaning through much use over many centuries. Third, such a contrast suggests that 'pastoral' is again somehow inferior to 'mission'. After centuries of affirming the value of the 'pastoral' nature of the church, it seems unwise to start using the word as a term to describe what we now need to leave behind.

It would seem better to look for terms where we can begin again to fill the words with content from the present in order to help us to get a handle on our situation. For this reason the words used here, though arguably less memorable, will hopefully be less misleading. The terms are related to the church as we know it, the *inherited* mode, and the church as it needs to be – and in places is becoming – namely the *emerging* church. The word inherited does remind us of the very considerable history behind the present ways of operating in the church. 'Emerging' reminds us that this is not about the imposition of some theory, but rather the observation of some developments which may well prove foundational in how the church is the church into the twenty-first century. There are occasions where the words 'maintenance', 'pastoral', and more so, 'missionary' remain valid terms to us, but the basic contrast being drawn is between the church in inherited mode and the church in emerging mode.

2

The Journey into Inherited Ways

> Most of us still live in the refuge of our parishes, which
> are more like the relics of an antiquated Christianity
> than the first fruits of a new people won for Christ in
> the midst of today's world.
>
> Jose Comblin, *Being Human*, p.26.

> The power of contentment over belief is universal.
>
> J.K. Galbraith, *The Culture of Contentment*, p.10.

Ask anyone to tell you about themselves and they will become
historical, they will start to tell you their story and the major milestones in their life.

What is true of individuals is true of nations, and of communities, such as the church. Indeed the history of literature is full of
great journeys. Epic journeys make great stories. From Homer's
Odyssey through Bunyan's *Pilgrim's Progress*, to *A Walk across
America*, the story of a great journey has the power to capture the
imagination and to communicate truth. Part of the power of
'journey' as a theme is its ability to bring together the varied
strands of life into one integrating whole. They connect with us
and our story; probably because life is like a journey. Journeys
speak to us because they express both process and progress. Yes,
there are great milestones reached and decisive turnings taken,
but journeys are set in the context of the humdrum, the ordinary
and the everyday. That is like life.

James Hopewell, in his seminal book, *Congregations*, has demonstrated clearly how important it is to understand the story of a church if you are to help to bring about change. Our story shapes us. It is for this reason, that in seeking to understand why the church functions as it does today, we need to know something of our history. *The past has shaped the present.* It has done so as the result of a long journey and unless we have some understanding of that story we are unlikely to be able to find ways of moving beyond the present. Considering the story of how the church came to function as it does will put us in a better place to identify the leading characteristics of a church that will take us on into the future.

The good and the best

Before proceeding to the story of how the *inherited ways* of being churches have come about there is one important point to be made. It is this, that the inherited model of church is far from being all bad news. Indeed, if it was, our task would be relatively easy. 'Off with the old and on with the new' would be the simple message, and everyone would immediately embrace it as good news. Life, unfortunately is just not that simple.

The truth is more like the following, admittedly simplified and overtidy, description of the present way of being church; namely that one third of its life is good and needs to be carried on into the future; one third is good, but needs to find new ways of being expressed; and one third is no longer relevant or useful.

It is important to affirm what is good about the inherited ways of being church. In the best sense it has often been truly pastoral. And to care you need to stop and be with people over a long period. Moreover, many church buildings, including many classic pieces of architecture which characterize and enrich our national landscape, point to the presence of the transcendent in our midst, even today. The many fine works of service, organized by and from the local church, have contributed disproportionately to the production of a caring culture and community. Such compassion witnesses to God's care of the environment and those who live and work in it. The provision of rites of passage, which typifies the church in 'inherited mode', speaks to people about a God who cares, because they experience a church which cares – well, on a good day anyway!

The need for fundamental change does not negate the faithful and caring work of thousands of church members up and down the country – many in quiet, unnoticed ways over the course of many years. The situation is rather like the problems which our shipbuilding industry faces today. As often as not there is a loyal, industrious and skilled workforce – part of a community whose history is steeped in shipmaking. Nonetheless, if the demand for ships is less or the ways they need to be designed, marketed and made are substantially different, then no amount of praise for the fine workforce will deal with the problem. Indeed one owes it to the workforce to spot trends as soon as possible and make the radical changes for their sake as well as their customers'. So too with the church. If the inherited pattern of being church is one that has served us well, and in which the church has been served well by many faithful generations of members, we owe it to those very people to be aware of the changes taking place. Otherwise, to use a different shipping analogy, the church may become, like some of the ancient seaports of England, stranded several miles inland as a result of silting up over many years.

With the use of these terms and the recognition of the good things we have inherited from the past, we are now ready to embark on the story of the long journey of the church into its present way of operating. That journey can best be told by pointing to five particular milestones or shaping events which have left a series of defining characteristics on the church as we now know it.

Hierarchical society and the loss of lay vitality

One of the earliest evidences of the church being shaped by the surrounding culture can be seen in the way that so quickly a strong hierarchical structure emerged. Certainly the New Testament shows clear evidence of the role of leadership, yet the sense of what today is called every-member ministry is very striking. Especially is this so when one considers the strong hierarchical and patriarchical nature of the surrounding culture. This lay-vitality (see 2 Corinthians 12-14, and the various lists of gifts and ministries in the Epistles) was certainly one of the striking features of the church in New Testament times. As Bishop John Robinson in his usual provocative style put it:

> One of the most remarkable facts in the history of religion is the astonishing and well-nigh total eclipse in the New Testament of the priestly side of the Old Testament religion . . . the *unpriestly* character of early Christianity must surely have been one of the first things to strike an outsider, whether he were Jew or pagan.[1]

Yet the fact remains that within a few decades of the completion of the New Testament documents, Clement, the Bishop of Rome, was writing 'Do nothing without the bishop.' The way the church operated was very quickly shaped by the impact of a hierarchical and patriarchal society. Hierarchy in the form of leadership is certainly needed in church and society. However, the church today is discovering that such leadership needs to be exercised in a collaborative, rather than a dictatorial, style. The sentiments of the Duke of Wellington, a great military leader turned politician in the nineteenth century are not what the church needs today. Writing to his niece after holding his first Cabinet meeting as Prime Minister he said: 'I held my first Cabinet meeting today. I gave them their orders, but they seemed to want to stay to discuss them!'

One of the signs of the vitality of the church in the twentieth century has been the recovery of the foundational role of laity, expressed alike in concepts such as 'every member ministry', and in the development of synodical structures of government. However, the church continues to be shaped by a concept of

[1] J. A. T. Robinson, *On Being the Church in the World*, p.72.

ministry inherited more from our cultural journey, than from the setting off point of the New Testament church with a sense of a whole community being energized and equipped by the Spirit to participate in God's mission.

The future will certainly entail a continued reworking of the imperial distortions of leadership, and rediscovery of all leadership as servant leadership. The financial constraints in which the church finds itself at present can be seen as divine shaping of the church to recover its Body nature, in a release of the creativity of the whole church. Certainly collaborative styles of leadership, and permission-giving styles of ministry, are marks of local churches which show evident vitality across the churchmanship spectrum.

In short, the impact of hierarchical societies has been to leave the church with the defining characteristic of its being a *clerical church*. The emerging church will, in contrast, be marked by lay *vitality*.

The shift from Celtic to Roman patterns and the loss of community

Two major pilgrimages will take place in 1997 as part of the nationwide Decade of Evangelism, for that year marks the fourteen hundredth anniversary of the death of St Columba, one of the most influential Celtic missionaries, and also the arrival in England of St Augustine of Canterbury who played a major part in shaping and forwarding the mission of the church at the time of the collapse of the Roman Empire.

Those two men and two events remind us that the Church in England is the inheritor of a long history. That history has shaped who we are and how the church is the church. Indeed, the handover of the baton of faith from the Celtic to the Roman Church (marked in many ways by the Synod of Whitby called together by St Hilda) introduces us to one of the earliest shaping events in the forming of our present way of being church.

The shift from Celtic to Roman mode in the life of the church was a process that took several centuries, but the change was profound. Celtic Christianity was established by wandering missionaries, typically among local communities. The wanderings of the Celtic missionaries are seen in their most dramatic form in the way that St Columba and others would get into their minute coracles on the northern coast of Ireland and set sail for wherever the Spirit might lead (blow) them. Hence the establishing of monasteries on Iona and other Scottish islands. Lindisfarne followed as a missionary centre. Celtic Christians seem to have felt most at home when they were all at sea!

The Roman way of being church grew out of very different soil. And it was definitely soil not sea in which it had been established. One of the lasting gifts to Western civilization of the Roman culture was its fine organization, seen alike in its buildings, roads and its administration. They were skilled organizers. Along with their legal system, it is the institutions of state and community that have strongly shaped the whole of our national life. The impact this has had on the church was to institutionalize it. From the free-flowing pattern of Celtic faith-communities established among the people, the church moved into the efficient organization we know today as the parish structure. Although there is a downside to this 'regimentation', it is important to acknowledge the missionary nature of this move. It was to ensure that every community (and so every person) was within reach of a church presence.

While there were clear gains from a settled geographical area of responsibility and mission, we need to recognize that the sense of community has often been lost through the focus of attention being on the church as an institution or organization. Whilst 'community' is of the essence of the New Testament Christianity, it is a word which is now associated in the church's vocabulary with monasticism and religious orders, and sometimes with extreme groupings within the church.

For most people, the church is one voluntary association alongside others, one of the many clubs or societal institutions to which they choose to belong. Further, we commonly think of Christian life from an individualistic or, at best, an organizational perspective, but rarely from a communal perspective.[2]

There are institutional aspects of the church, but we distort the nature of the faith community if we make those aspects the primary or sole way of seeing the church. Most churches today are not, in this sense 'communities'. The development of home groups has been a move within the church designed to restore the relational element in the life of the church. However, all too often we have to admit that what started as a 'new way of being church' has become simply a whole new set of meetings to attend – a new level of organization.

In a culture which seems to have something close to an allergy to anything institutional, it is vital that the church finds ways of expressing its life in simpler and lighter ways. The parish system has served the church well in continually alerting it to its mission to the whole community and to the structures of education and welfare within that area. However, we will need to continue to be committed to the principle of service to the wider community whilst learning to be flexible about how it is achieved. This is so not least since the sense of 'local community' is being continually eroded.

The result of this long process has been that we understand the church as *parish church*, working in a defined geographical and social grouping. The emerging church will need, like the Celtic Church of the past to find ways of being church through *networks of relationships*.

The Reformation loss of a missionary perspective

The church which emerged out of the Reformation in the sixteenth century was a church powerfully shaped by a Christendom model of society. In this perspective, the whole of society was seen as 'under God' – and as far as possible 'under the church'. Although that gave to the whole society a common set of Christian values – such as national laws largely shaped by the ten commandments –

[2] John Westerhoff III, *Living the Faith Community*, p.10.

it did significantly blunt the missionary nature of the church. The whole community, society and nation, were viewed as Christian; virtually everybody was baptized, which only confirmed the Christian nature of the whole society. Nor was such a view unique to England; Calvin's Switzerland and Luther's Germany were both established as 'Christian communities' in the sense of 'Christian nations'. This left little or no work of mission or evangelism to be done. Indeed, as David Bosch puts it:

> Lutheran orthodoxy believed that the 'Great Commission' had been fulfilled by the apostles and was no longer binding on the church.[3]

Even when the church did awaken, in the eighteenth and nineteenth centuries, to its missionary task, it is striking to note that it turned its attention 'o'er heathen lands afar' as the appropriate place for it to engage in mission.

Nearer to home, the Church of England was conceived as a church in pastoral mode, and has grown that way since its earliest days. When we inquire of the Book of Common Prayer about the Church of England's doctrine of evangelism, we find that the only reference to evangelism is in the Preface of the 1662 book. There it is explained that the service for the Baptism of those of Riper Years was introduced as 'always useful for the baptizing of Natives in our Plantations'. This is hardly an adequate or appropriate theology of evangelism for the church at the end of the twentieth century! Whatever the validity of the setting of the church in 1662, we certainly cannot now begin from the notion that Church and Society are coterminous.

Whilst retaining, and indeed strengthening, the sense of mission to the whole community, the church needs today to face the fact that a Christian worldview and value-system is no longer the norm in the UK. Our starting point here must be that we are now in a mission situation ourselves; for that, the whole church needs to be reorientated around mission.

[3] David Bosch, *Transforming Mission*, p.249.

Enlightenment worldview marginalizing values

Whilst the church has been in England for almost the whole of the Christian era (earliest evidences point to Christianity taking root before A.D. 100), the Church of England is not yet five hundred years old. Throughout its history it has functioned in a ferment of ideas begun in the Renaissance, and continued in the Enlightenment era of Western Europe. The emerging of the questioning, scientific mind, feeling increasing freedom from the church in its search for an understanding of all that is, has been the backdrop to the whole of the life of the Church of England. This has had a profound effect on the philosophical framework within which the church has sought to do her work. As Os Guinness observed:

> Christianity is like the majestic ruins of an ancient cathedral from which stones are plundered for the construction of countless other buildings. Politicians quarry from her vocabulary, psychiatrists dip into its treasury of practices and symbols, and advertisers mimic the resonances of its acoustics. Each pillager uses just what is convenient. But the decisiveness and authority of any distinctive Christian truth are gone.[4]

The church, and individuals in it, have often retreated from the public arena to the safety of a personal (and private) religion, and to the security of the church as an Ark. I heard recently of a Christian in hospital suffering from cancer. She said that half the ward fled when the chaplain came. However, the other half stayed hoping he would come and talk with them about 'ultimate' and 'spiritual' issues and their fear of death which they did not want to 'burden or embarrass' their family with. Sadly, although he did have a word with them all, he restricted himself to social chat at which he was very skilled. If that is true of the paid 'purveyors of religion', how much more is it often true of the 'silent adherents'? Religion has become marginalized and privatized in our culture. As two modern writers have put it:

[4] Os Guinness, *The Gravedigger File*, p.212.

The success of science also precipitated a religious crisis. As the physical evidence for religion was stripped away by successive generations of scientists, faith turned inwards to find a safe refuge inside the self.[5]

Many of us today live in a kind of inner apartheid. We segregate out a small corner of pious activities and then can make no sense out of the rest of our lives.[6]

This marginalizing and privatizing of values, beliefs and activities have pushed the church into being what seems to many outside its doors as simply a *religious club* – a place where religion rather than golf is the leisure activity which draws people to take part in its activities. This has resulted in many within the church finding themselves unable to find words with which to convey to 'outsiders' the faith enjoyed 'within'. The emerging church will need a *whole-life focus* and a spirituality that enables it to meet with God in the whole of life, not just 'within' either the self or the church.

Loss of distinctives in the twentieth-century Western Church

When the end-of-term report comes to be written on the Church in the West in the twentieth century, it will have to include, on the negative side, the phrase 'failure of nerve'. There has been a serious loss of argument with the Enlightenment worldview. The critical approach to Scripture, psychology, evolution, all found the church unable to stem the tide of a secular, materialistic worldview as the framework in which the people of our culture see reality. There has been a consequent loss of gospel content in such evangelism as has been attempted. William Abraham describes the weakness in these terms:

At the very best, most modern evangelism hands over two

[5] Bryan Appleyard, *Understanding the Present*, p.227.
[6] Richard Foster, *Prayer*, p.179.

things: deeply reduced fragments of the Christian message and the personalistic debris of the Christian moral tradition.[7]

In similar vein, Richard Lovelace writes:

Evangelism-in-Depth and two-by-two house evangelism can expand the trade routes of the gospel outside our church walls, but unless what we export is more than a two-dimensional caricature of Christian spirituality, we will not overcome the credibility gap among consumers.[8]

Moreover, this failure of nerve has been seen in the loss of Christian distinctives and the essentially counter-culture nature of the faith. Yet the very subversive nature of acknowledging Jesus as Lord was crucial to the church's evangelization of the Roman Empire. Today's church member is always eager to show that 'Christians are normal, that Christians can have fun, that Christians can . . .' Valid and understandable though such sentiments are they are strikingly different from Paul's call to the Ephesians, or the words of Jesus in the Sermon on the Mount.[9] Those passages positively celebrate the difference knowing God makes to personal moral values and lifestyle. A missionary church, though deeply involved in the whole of society, will yet be courageously distinctive from it. It will see itself as called to live by prophetic *counter-values*.

The point is well illustrated by the blandness of the contemporary church's use of the Lord's Prayer as compared with its perception and use in the early centuries of the church's life:

Allegiance to the empire was determined by proclaiming the kingship of the emperors, the holiness of their names, and submission to their will. To declare otherwise, as demanded by praying the Our Father, was to act subversively towards the powers and principalities.[10]

[7] William Abraham, *The Logic of Evangelism*, p.141.
[8] Richard Lovelace: *The Dynamics of Spiritual Life*, p.236
[9] Ephesians 4:17-19, and Matthew 5:11-16.
[10] Michael Crosby, *Thy Will be Done* (subtitled: *Praying the Our Father as Subversive Activity*).

Characteristics of the inherited way of being church

Having travelled this journey with the church we are in a position to draw some conclusions about they key characteristics of the church as we know it today. It is helpful to identify those marks under a series of different elements. When we come to explore the *emerging* church we will then be able to use those same elements in order to draw comparisons and distinctions.

In terms of its *basic structure* the local church in *inherited* mode has a relatively *fixed and unwieldy* form. Moreover, as so often happens in institutions which have a long history, the original reason for doing something is obscured. The practice is maintained long after the original reason has ceased to apply, or been forgotten. An example of that is the story of a women's group in a church which always ended its meetings promptly at 3.15p.m. When enquiry was made as to why that time was so special it was discovered that the meetings were timed to end then so that mothers could collect their children as they came out of school at 3.30p.m. A sensible plan – until it is pointed out that the youngest member of the group was over seventy-five years old. Not only had the children all now left school but the grandchildren too. Practices tend to develop a life of their own independent of the value and original purpose. Similarly the practice of holding two services on Sunday, at 11a.m. and 6.30p.m. almost certainly arose out of the need to cater for the contrasting needs of 'upstairs and downstairs'.

Our contemporary setting is, contrastingly, much more interested in travelling light, stripping operations down to the basic essentials and identifying the purpose before assessing the value of any action and routine.

As far as *leadership style* is concerned the inherited mode retains what could be described as a strongly *clerical* form. Clergy play a dominant and controlling role. This includes the provider/client relationship in the congregation, kept in being by a tendency in clergy to 'need to be needed', and a preference among many congregations to be passive recipients of priestly activity. The great problem with such a style is that it reinforces passive attitudes to faith and discipleship, works best with those who want to settle for a quiet life and frustrates those who have the vision and energy to do creative things themselves. Yet, the most vital and almost limitless renewal resources of any operation, are the creativity and commitment of all those involved. We certainly need a more enabling, empowering and collaborative style of leadership if the church is to connect with ordinary people today.

Associated with this last characteristic is the tendency in the inherited mode for the *pastoral* work to be geared to keeping people *happy*. Comfort is a key factor. Many come to church looking to have their ills soothed. The experience of many churches, for example, which have set up home groups is that when personal needs are focused upon then, like Parkinson's Law, 'needs expand to fill time available'. J. K. Galbraith identifies this as a primary characteristic of Western society:

> There is an eager market for that which pleases and reassures.[11]

Such a church has its *focus* on church-life issues. It develops a strong life of its own, but at the price of becoming disconnected from the world around. In such a church the church role which a person fills is seen as having more significance than his or her everyday life and work. A bishop was recently introduced to a member of a church he was visiting as 'one of our senior servers'. Fortunately someone told the bishop that, when not at church, this person was head of town planning for one of the largest conurbations in the UK. The inherited mode of operating as a church all too easily lapses into that unbalanced perspective. Church becomes a world of its own.

A further characteristic of the Church in inherited mode is that it *functions* basically as an *organization*. Any understanding of the Church as community takes second place to the practical management of an organization. Rules, precedent and power

---

[11] J.K. Galbraith, *The Culture of Contentment*, p.2.

become crucial dynamics in such a situation.

The inherited *model* of church assumes that there is a *single* way of being church. That model colours and shapes everyone's ideas of what we mean by church. This happens even where the opportunity to try different patterns is very clear. So, for example, where the church has collapsed in an area, such as an inner city housing estate, the temptation is to have a vision for the revival of the church which includes all the traditional elements such as PCC meetings and minutes, secretaries, churchwardens, lay readers, robed choir, uniformed organizations, and, of course, church building with spire.

That one single way of being church can be summed up in the formula:

$$church = building + priest + stipend$$

The very use of the word 'church' underlines this formula. People talk about 'going to church' when they are speaking about the church *building*. They also talk about 'going into the church' when they are referring to the *ordained ministry*. There is no equivalent popular use of the word church which expresses the fact that the church is primarily a community rather than a building or clergy person. It may well be that such a use of the word 'church' to mean 'community' will emerge. This does not mean that the church will sell its buildings, or sack all its clergy. Rather, the case is being made for seeing that the *church as community* is likely to be what the church is increasingly seen to be.

Finally, the church in inherited mode is *orientated* around the *past*. This is one of the great paradoxes of the Christian faith – and probably of all religions. The mission becomes a movement and turns into a monument. It needs itself continually to be evangelized.

Christians obediently follow a man who himself obediently followed no one. They believe in a system at the centre of which is a man who broke with the system which he

17 John Hull, *What Prevents Christian Adults from Learning?* p.78.

inherited . . . Christians become followers of this imaginative and creative Jesus by carefully suppressing innovation and creativity.[12]

It can be argued that John Hull in the above quotation overstates the case, for the radical Jesus also said he did not come to abolish but fulfil. Nonetheless, his way of fulfilling was radical, not least because through the preaching of the kingdom, it was orientated around the future rather than around the past.

In the context of the culture in which we live it is vital that the church finds a way of ordering its life around participating in the search for hope and for the creation of a 'civlization of love'. That is where our culture is looking. It is into that situation that the Christian message of hope, resurrection, kingdom and the End must be given expression in the life of the local church.

An abiding lesson

We have traced the journey of the church over the period of a millennium and a half, and have noted some of the major milestones of that journey. One particular observation needs to be noted, for it applies to how the church seeks to be the church in the future.

The fact is that each time the church has been through a major change, it has been as a result of the changing culture and context in which it was operating at the time. (Certainly, the changes we have considered were all related to the changes taking place in the surrounding culture.) In view of the considerable changes taking place in our culture today it would be surprising if a further change were not to take place. Indeed, such a change is not only needed, it has already been called for by Lambeth 88. Moreover, at least in its 'green shoots of recovery' form, such changes can already be seen.

The fact is that the 'church' is continually adapting to the movements within the surrounding culture, and for its own health – as well as the fulfilment of its mission – it needs to continue that process. Tracing this journey can therefore be a great encouragement to the church to keep moving and alive to the Spirit as it seeks to discern how God is calling it today. The shape of that call will relate closely to the changing patterns and forms of modern culture. It is to an understanding of the culture in which the church is set that we turn next.

3

Culture Shift as Context for Mission

The human race finds itself today in a new period of her history, characterized by profound and accelerated changes which progressively extend to the entire universe.

Vatican II, The Church in the Modern World No.4.

Seek the peace and prosperity of the city to which I have carried you into exile. Pray to the Lord for it, because if it prospers you too will prosper.

Jeremiah 29:7.

The first task of a missionary church is to understand the culture to which it is sent. Normally that means learning a new language, understanding strange social customs and discovering how to interpret special nuances of body language, verbal emphases and social habits as vital channels of communication.

For the church in England this is a particularly hard task. After all, if you go to a strange country and society, the very strangeness is continually drawing attention to the things that strike you as unique, puzzling and different to your own culture. But when you seek to go to your own culture in mission, the culture itself seems to disappear, for it is part of you and you are part of it. I discovered this truth in a trip a few years ago to California. We were visiting Death Valley and went into the Information Centre and selected some of the more striking photographs to bring home. As I offered my money to the man behind the counter I heard him say, 'Say, gee, I sure like your accent.' I looked around to see who he was talking to, only to see that my wife and I were the only people there. He was talking to me! It was the day I discovered that I had an accent. As I reflected on the experience later I realized that all my life I had thought that I spoke normally – other people had accents. Being a 'home missionary' is a hard task but a vital one.

We know only too well how the church in its mission to continents such as Africa and South America, have done much harm – to cultures and to the gospel – by the imposition of a foreign culture in the name of the gospel. As one African tellingly put it: 'You have brought us the gospel *and* your culture, and have required of us that we become white men in a black man's skin.'

The good news is that there are people coming to our aid just at this point. People who are helping the Church to distinguish between what is 'gospel' and what is 'culture' in our own society. Bishop Lesslie Newbigin is one person who has been at the forefront of such thinking. After several decades of missionary work in India he returned home to England enabled to see it as a 'foreign culture' and to gain insight into the distinction between 'gospel' and 'culture'. Graham Cray, principal of Ridley Hall Theological College, is another person helping the Church – largely as a result of his involvement in and understanding of the Rock music culture – to 'read the times' (as distinct from *The Times*!)[1]

Beginning with symptoms

For the great majority of ordinary Christians who do not have much interest in sociology or philosophy, consideration of 'issues of culture' may seem irrelevant and something best left to the experts. However, a moment's thought will alert us to the fact that the changes taking place around us profoundly affect our lives, particularly the lives of the under-thirties.

[1] 'From Here to Where?' Board of Mission Occasional Paper, obtainable from Board of Mission, Church House, Great Smith Street, London SW1P 3NZ.

Consider, for example, attitudes to, and patterns of, sexual activity. The older generation have always complained about the immorality of the young. However, there is now clear statistical evidence, reinforced by the experience of most people from somewhere within the wider circle of relatives, that young people have a very different way of seeing sexual experience from that of previous generations. That view is well expressed in a recent Report produced by the Health and Welfare Unit of the IEA (Institute for Economic Affairs), in which it is said:

> ... The approved pattern is one of individual entrepreneurs, each free to strike a bargain as producer of sexual gratification with any willing consumer.[2]

Although the IEA is a somewhat unlikely source for prophetic insight, it certainly is right in pointing out how far the consumer mentality now permeates our whole way of thinking. Consumer culture is alive and well – even in bed!

Another usual bone of contention between the generations is the attitude of the young to authority and authority figures. Here we see not just normal generational conflict, but rather a youth culture which is starting from a very different worldview. Addressing a recent European Conference of Catholic Bishops, Cardinal Basil Hume said:

> In a world that is seen by many to have no ultimate purpose or value, the Self is seen as providing the only realm in which our experience can have meaning. No authority eternal to the individual is acknowledged.[3]

Such profound shifts in perceptions of the nature of the world, life and human values, remind me of an incident that took place whilst taking my grandson (then aged five) out for a walk. We were walking along a wooded path when we passed a small, somewhat hidden, electricity substation. He asked me what it was. Reaching

[2] Norman Dennis and George Erdos, *Families without Fatherhood*, p.66.
[3] Ruth Gledhill Report in *The Times*, 1993.

to the fringes of my scientific and electrical knowledge I told him
that it took the electricity from the power station and made it suitable for distribution to people's homes. Wanting to avoid further
questioning which might take me out of my depth, I did what
most older people do. I retreated into the familiar world of history
and began to talk about the days before electricity. I asked him if
he knew how people lit their homes before electricity had been
invented. He thought for a while and then said 'candles'.
Proceeding further, on both the walk and the conversation, I
pointed out that you need electricity to make a TV work, and that
'when Grandpa was growing up, we did not have TV.' First he
asked, 'Why not?', so I explained that it had not yet been invented
(well not yet sufficiently marketed actually). 'Why not?' he asked.
That was more difficult to answer. Then, stopping in his tracks as
the truth sank in, he looked straight at me and said, 'Well, what did
you watch?' His view of reality shaped his understanding of
'another world'.

His misunderstanding simply created some amusement for the
rest of the family. However, the church is in danger of doing just
the same as it looks into the present and the future through the
distorting lenses of our inherited culture. Some of that inherited
expression of the faith may indeed be gospel truth, some may
simply be outmoded or distorted cultural expression. If the next
generation is to grasp and enter the faith, we will need to do some
work so as to understand what is going on around us. Unless we
do that we will be in danger of reading back our view of the world
into a totally different situation.

Christian culture

We have already seen that the Christian message, and the church's
lifestyle, have been skilled in adapting to new culture. This means
that the church should be well situated to understand the
profound changes taking place today and to make creative adjust-
ments to those changes.

The Christian faith has been up to the challenge of such changes over two millennia of missionary adaptation. Yes, there have been adaptations to culture which have sold the gospel short. The historic Creeds of the church were largely forged as a response to undue adaptation in the form of heresy. At other times the church has risked the gospel by its refusal to adapt to change. When that happens it becomes simply an antiquarian ghetto. Nonetheless, the gospel has been taken to an extraordinarily rich diversity of cultures and survived as an expression of all that is most authentic about that culture. Gathering together, even if only in one's mind's eye, an Italian Jesuit priest, a Bolivian Pentecostal peasant, an Anglican stockbroker from the City of London and a member of the Maori Church, can be a wonderful picture of the richness and diversity which God has given his church. It gives the church today a sense of confidence when, like Abraham, we face the unknown journey ahead of us.

Culture shift

We have considered just two 'presenting symptoms' of the different perspectives abroad in society today, namely the consumer mentality which now affects sexual morality and the individualism that rejects all external authority. Before proceeding to explore the underlying factors it is important to note something so obvious that it could pass us by, namely that we are in a period of profound cultural shift.

Culture, like any plant or person, is a living thing and is changing, adapting and growing all the time. However, one can also detect in history great upheavals and shifts that represent fundamental changes and a whole new beginning. These are moments of major cultural shift. The collapse of the Roman Empire and formation of Christendom was one such moment. Another was the period of the Reformation and Renaissance in the sixteenth century. A further upheaval can be identified at the end of the eighteenth century with the emergence of what is called the Age of Enlightenment. Each of these major scene changes took at least fifty and sometimes more than a hundred years to emerge as

a definable new expression of human culture. Those three dominant marks of Western civilization have been labelled, succes-
sively, Christendom, Renaissance and Enlightenment. Observers
today seem to be of one mind that we are in another such major
cultural upheaval. Thomas Merton, a Trappist Monk, said:

> We are living in the greatest revolution in history, a huge,
> spontaneous upheaval of the entire human race. Not a rev-
> olution planned and carried out by any particular party, race
> or nation, but a deep elemental boiling over of all the inner
> contradictions that have ever been in people, a revolution of
> the chaotic forces inside everybody. This is not something we
> have chosen nor is it anything we are free to avoid.[4]

One of the clearest evidences that we are right in the midst of such
a major shift is the fact that the word 'post' is attached to so many
of the characteristics of what observers see in our society. We are
told that we live, variously, in a post-scientific, post-Industrial,
post-Christian, post-Christendom, post-Enlightenment and post-
modern world. That suggests we had better be clear what we
mean by 'post-anything'. The word needs to be understood in
three ways.

'Post' points to the fact that society is moving on beyond something. 'Post' means simply 'after', as in 'post-natal' or 'post-
operative'. Using the prefix 'post' also points to something more
subtle than a total abandonment of the past. A 'post-graduate',
hopefully does not forget or ignore his or her education. Indeed
when a job is advertised as suitable for such a person, it is expected
that they will take their past learning with them. That is what they
have to contribute. Equally, a 'post-scientific' or 'post-Enlightenment' culture will assuredly take into the future many of the
tremendous advances which have come to human society through
the 'scientific' era. None of us wishes to disinvent aesthetics, air
travel or antibiotics – and that is just from the first letter of the
alphabet! 'Post' in this sense implies continuity with, and building

[4] Quoted by Diarmuid O'Murchu, in *Our World in Transition*, p.7.

on, the past, yet going beyond into something else.

'Post-anything', however, alerts us to what we do not know. Under the guise of sounding philosophical, as the words post-Enlightenment and post-modernism sound, these terms are a tacit admission that we do not know what is coming. Such terms tell us where we have come from, but in the telling are actually admitting that we do not yet know where we are going to. The future is yet to be. Its shape is unclear. We are in a period of transition. Bearing in mind that such periods of major change take at least fifty years to come about, it is almost certain that anyone reading this book will spend the rest of his or her life in this transition period.

In terms of the life of the church that means we will have to be bilingual; speaking the language of where we have come from as well as learning the language of the new order of reality into which our society is entering. It may well mean that we will need two or more ways of being church. One which relates to those who belong to the old order and one or more relating to those who inhabit the new order. What the church needs to be aware of is that most of the present church members belong to the old, disappearing, way of seeing reality. Both for sheer survival and certainly for the effective pursuit of our missionary call, the church will need to find ways of relating the gospel and the life of the church to those whose lives have been shaped by that emerging perspective – hence the need for an 'emerging church'.

So what is the shape of the *emerging* culture with which the church is to engage? There are many ways of describing it, but simply taking up a series of key words will help us get within the perspective of such a worldview more quickly than any other approach. It may also help us to realize how far most of us are already shaped by that emerging culture.

The individual

A remarkable shift has taken place in humanity's understanding of the universe and our place in it since the days when it was thought that the sun was in orbit around the earth. At that time, although the earth was thought to be the centre of the universe, there was a clear conviction that a Supreme Being existed before whom we were called to live out our lives and to whom in the final issue we were accountable.

Since Copernicus and others discovered that the earth rotates around the sun, that the sun is not at the centre of our galaxy and that our galaxy is not near any 'centre' of the universe (if such a location exists), people have come increasingly to see themselves as the centre. Bryan Appleyard argues that this has come about as science, seeking to be 'objective', excluded the 'observing self' from its calculations. The marginalized 'self' then found a way back into the picture via the centre of its own universe.

> The self is denied its place in the world and its source of values. Its resorts, finally, to a pagan act devoted to its own cultivation and worship.[5]

Descartes famous saying 'I think, therefore I am' (cogito, ergo sum) is considered to have had a formative influence on modern society, shaping the lives of millions who have never heard either of him or his dictum. However, it is more likely that his influence is due more to his being able to articulate a widespread intuition than that he taught a whole culture to think differently. The fact remains that the self is now seen as the centre of the universe and its own seat of authority. New Age spirituality exactly fits this perception, teaches that 'I am my own divinity', thus making the individual, rather like a spacecraft, a totally self-contained and sealed unit trying to find its way and its home in an alien universe. In this connection it is interesting to see how the very word 'individual' has changed in meaning.

> The word individual has gone through a revolution of meaning. Coming from the Latin *individuus*, indivisible, it was once used to emphasize that we are joined together: as individuals we are inseparable. Now it stresses the exact

opposite, namely that each person is an indivisible whole, existing as a distinct entity.[6]

The consequence of this shift is that individualism is a key characteristic of the culture in which we live. What is the Christian response to such a development?

In terms of its implied affirmation of the value of the individual, such a development can be welcomed. Moreover, the process of becoming consciously 'one's own person' (called 'individuation' by psychologists) seems to connect with the worth of the individual so strongly expressed by Jesus Christ in his ministry and by the Apostle Paul in the way that he wrote about the church as the place where each member was valued – for their own unique contribution. Where the Christian, and indeed much modern psychology, would want to point to another perspective is that we are not only manifestly 'social beings', but that by our very nature we are 'beings-in-relationship'. This is expressed in the social nature of God as Trinity, and is a major theme of a range of modern theologians.[7] We are not sealed units but part of a committed community. Independence is a stage on the road to maturity which itself is marked by interdependence. However, the church will not be able to communicate this, or any other aspect of its message, by recourse to authority, whether the church or the Bible. Individuals will need to choose freely to fulfil themselves by transcending the limits of their own separateness if they are to enter the fullest expression of our individuality in community and communion.

The Christian message is a call to go beyond the self in order to fulfil that self; not a call to submit to some external authority. Brian Keenan in the midst of suffering and profound oppression discovered the need for this 'outer-directedness' as the basis of survival:

[6] John Adair, *Effective Teambuilding*, p.53.
[7] Leonardo Boff, *Trinity and Society:* Colin Gunton, *The Promise of Trinitarian Theology* Jurgen Moltmann, *The Trinity and the Kingdom of God*: John Zizoulas, *Being as Communion*. See Robin Greenwood, *Transforming Priesthood*, Chapters four and five, for an application of this to the life of the church and the nature of Christian ministry.

I needed to commit and focus my inner understanding and strength outside myself.[8]

The whole

'Holistic' is one of the great buzz words of today. It expresses a deep instinct in human nature to find some way of integrating life. Physicists speak about the search for a 'theory of everything'. It is the same longing to find an organizing framework for all of life. This is what the Christian means by saying that mankind is a worshipping creature searching for some focus to life.

Such a search has been provoked by our analytical scientific culture. Science has done incredible work in its analysis of the universe, both as seen through the telescope and as seen through the microscope. However, in our taking things apart to see how they work, we have also lost an understanding of how things fit together again. Our whole culture is like many of us experienced in childhood and beyond, of taking something apart. By the time we have reassembled the thing we discover that we had a number of spare items left over and that the machine or toy did not work.

A deeper factor at work here is that the physics developed by Newton was a very mechanical way of seeing reality. It explained all the laws and mechanism that made it work. Relativity, quantum physics and chaos theory have all introduced us to a much less mechanical view of reality. One of the interesting effects of this mechanical, cause and effect and problem/solution approach to life has been the advent of the detective novel. It sets life down as essentially a problem to be solved. It is the form that the novel has taken during the rise of this way of seeing the world. It is symptomatic of a culture which sees life as a problem to be solved rather than a gift to be received and enjoyed with wonder and thanksgiving.

However, a major movement in our culture today is the desire to find out how to put things back together. The whole Green move-

[8] Brian Keenan, *An Evil Cradling*, p.252.

ment is part of this process, as is the interest in 'holistic medicine' and indeed the considerable interest in spirituality as evidenced by the New Age movement.

Christians can welcome this return to a more Biblical world-view, though we also need to challenge some of the 'holistic' moves not only because they lead directly to the occult, but because in rejecting an overrational approach to life, they proceed by way of rejecting the rational and the use of the mind. Leanne Payne is one author[9] who has written perceptively about what she calls the modern split between head and heart, mind and spirit. Christian faith is certainly committed to an integration of the varied aspects of our human nature.

This is one point at which the church in inherited mode is at a serious disadvantage, for it has often capitulated to the marginalizing of faith and a fragmented view of reality. It is suffering from the 'inner apartheid' of which Richard Foster writes.[10] The recovery of a holistic view of reality is essential to both the health of the church and to the forwarding of the work of mission. It will involve a rediscovery of how, in a pluralistic culture, we are to proclaim Jesus as Lord of all.

Purpose

A sense of meaning, significance and purpose in life are essential to healthy human existence in any age. However, a number of factors have produced a particular search for purpose in today's culture.

The scientific project has focused on the mechanics of life and in the process of explaining the mechanics has often lost touch with the sense of wonder, of the sacred, and of ultimate meaning. Down to the minutest details of all our bodily functions, particularly the sexual ones, we have an almost complete and total mechanical explanation. This then tends to rob us of any sense of freely chosen actions or real moral freedom.

[9] Leanne Payne, *The Healing Presence*, and other books.
[10] See quotation on p24 from his book, *Prayer*.

The moral freedom in our society that allows that almost 'anything goes' has meant that we are now searching for any way of finding out which is the best/right way. I can do my own thing, but is there anything that has real value for me to participate in?

The focus on the material (what can be seen and measured as well as what can be produced and possessed) has left an inner vacuum. When we are told that there may soon be 'an upturn in the economy' the question is raised as to whether a few more cars on the road and pounds in the bank are what life is about. Into this vacuum has come a search for meaning through the spiritual dimension. It is interesting that two very different women who expressed the materialism of the eighties, namely Samantha Fox and Shirley Conran, have recently returned to the headlines because of their public search for the lost spiritual dimension of life. Though they could be considered to have 'dropped out' of the eighties' values, it may well be that they are actually icons of the nineties' woman and man: searching for meaning, significance and purpose. The explosion of self-help literature is a further evidence of this contemporary hunger.

Certainly the Christian gospel with its call to participate in God's (mission) purpose for the whole of creation, has much to say to such a search as we shall see in greater detail later on.

Culture shaping

There are three particular responses that the Christian Church should make to such major shifts in our modern culture.

First we must understand it. That does not mean that everyone should be reading philosophy and physics. It does mean that the church needs to be reading the signs of the times. As the Old Testament puts it:

> The men of Issachar understood the times and knew what Israel should do.[11]

---

[11] 1 Chronicles 12:32.

Maybe each local church needs to set up a Neighbourhood Watch Group, not to protect each other's property, but rather in order to listen, reflect on and hear the heartbeat and the cry of the community. It is interesting how many evangelists today are identifying *listening* as one of the keys to evangelism.[12] It is there, of course, in the greatly increased emphasis on *process* approaches to evangelism as most of them give importance to people being listened to and their real questions being addressed. Indeed the agendas of some such groups are written by the members of the group.

Second, the church needs to be living the answers. The church needs to be not just discussing, but rather demonstrating, the answers to today's questions which the world is asking, not least because the church is part of that wider community and shares the same struggles and concerns. It is this that will best proclaim the good news – a community living by its truth in a way that demonstrates its answers to issues facing contemporary society.

Third, the church must then address these questions. It stands to reason that the church should not be addressing the issues people are not facing but the ones that do concern them. Often, however, the church will need to do this by addressing the 'question behind the question'. Approaching the work of evangelism from the position, for example, of saying 'I want to tell you how the sin issue in your life can be dealt with by Christ' is likely to be met by the assertion that the person does not have a sin problem. We have to come at truth through the doors that are open, rather than by attempting to blast holes through well-built walls.

Fourth, the church is to participate in the search for a new order in society. We saw earlier that a 'post-anything' culture is searching for a new framework in which to understand life. It is not sufficient for the church to work out how to survive, or even grow, in such a setting. Our calling is to participate in God's compassion for the whole creation. This is a major mark of a missionary church. It

[12] An excellent new course for small groups designed to equip people for a listening approach to life and to evangelism has recently been produced by Acorn Trust, entitled *Ears to Hear*.

is what is involved in participating in God's mission in the world, for the search is itself part of the moving of the Holy Spirit within our culture. The emerging church, in other words, will be one which participates in the shaping of the emerging culture.

> We are called to be physicians of that civilization about which we dream, the civilization of love.[13]

The same calling was expressed well by the Anglican Conference on Mission when it said:

> The church may choose to be a spectator at the birth of a new age, but is she not the one midwife capable of bringing forth a safe delivery?[14]

Indeed, this travail of which Paul speaks[15] itself points to the hope of a new beginning.

> Why are the sufferings of this world so reminiscent of birth pangs? Because a real birth is occurring. A new creation is about to come to light, a new world is being born.[16]

This is the task of a missionary church. This is why understanding the culture in which we are set is fundamental to the life of the church. It is the glorious vision that should inspire the church in and through all the upheavals it is experiencing in its own life, and in the life of the culture in which it is set. This is the journey that the church is called upon to make to the heavenly city, the new Jerusalem. It is a pilgrimage of adventure.

It requires that the church makes the journey from the guard's van of society into the vanguard. Instead of being at the rear, for ever looking back mournfully at disappearing mountain peaks or frantically pulling on the brake to slow down the pace of change, the church is called upon to be the pioneers of a new way of living.

[13] Pope Paul VI, *Address on December 31st, 1975.*
[14] MISAG II, *Towards Dynamic Mission*, p.6.
[15] Romans 8:18-27 and Galatians 4:19.
[16] Jose Comblin, *Being Human.* p.173.

The true attractiveness of the New Testament Church was the inner vitality which enabled it to live the answers to the questions people were asking. Our calling is no less, no different, nor – by God's grace – any less attainable.

THE CHURCH IN
EMERGING MODE

4

Objections to Missionary Congregations

... upsetting the existing order is dangerous business.
                    Melba Maggay, *Transforming Society*, p.86.

The command to love one another is not a domestic
policy of the church. It is its foreign policy.
                    John Drane, *Evangelism for a New Age*, p.164.

Before considering how new ways of being church might be
brought into being, it is important to face some substantial objections to the whole idea. These objections are expressed as criticisms of the idea of missionary congregations, so for the
purposes of this chapter, it will be necessary to revert to that
terminology. These counter-arguments need to be faced for
several reasons. They have a validity in themselves which
warrants their being addressed. Moreover, there are some
important insights which they express that can protect new
ways of being church from a number of pitfalls. The aim of this
chapter is to face the questions, provide some answers but also
to mine, out of the searching objections, truths that can both
protect and enrich the new models of church which are developing.

These objections group themselves into three categories. Some
question the desirability of 'the missionary congregation'. Others
doubt that they are achievable, and yet others suspect that even if

they are desirable and achievable, they simply cannot be sustained long term. We will look at each of these objections in turn.

Are they desirable?

One of the great strengths, glories, and distinctives of the Anglican Church is that it sees itself as a church to and for the whole community, not as a gathered church. The notion of missionary congregation, indeed the very word congregation, seems to smack of congregationalism, of a gathered church, ghetto mentality. As such is that not a sure sign of the final withdrawal of the church into the shell of itself and its self-consciousness – all in the name of mission?

Reality is in fact more subtle and, potentially, more creative. The basis of the parish-church versus gathered-church divide is rooted deeply in the history of the church. The Christendom/ Reformation model of church was one that saw the church as coterminous with society, which is hardly surprising since practically everybody was baptized. It was against this that the Anabaptists revolted, shaping the church around the gathering of the faithful. History has however moved on since then. Neither model, especially in the caricatured form in which they so often are presented, are viable options for today. A church that is indistinguishable from the local community and coterminous with it is a church that has virtually disappeared from view; it has nothing distinctive about itself, nor any message to speak. Of what value is a church that has nothing to say? Equally a gathered church that is not rooted in, and part of, a local community, although it may well have a strong and distinctive message, actually has no one to address. Of what value is a church that has something vital to say, but no one to say it to? As Robin Greenwood puts it:

> . . . a church that does indeed exist for the entire community simultaneously needs to know its own identity.[1]

[1] Robin Greenwood, *Transforming Priesthood*, p.135.

Furthermore non-conformist churches today have a strong sense of commitment to the local community – sometimes it is stronger than the commitment of the local Anglican Church. Equally Anglican churches are increasingly 'gathered' today. The fact that giving in real terms is going up whilst attendance figures continue to decline is clear evidence of a recognizable group of 'committed' members.

Any church worth its salt[2], will, like an ellipse, have two focal points (see figure one below). The simplest way to draw an ellipse it to put two drawing pins into a piece of card and place a loop of string around them (as represented by the outline of the triangle in the diagram). By putting a pencil in the top of the loop and allowing it to go completely round one way an ellipse will be drawn. That drawing will trace out a multitude of different triangles all having the same base line drawn between two focal points.

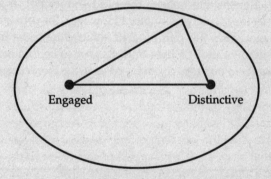

Figure one: the double focus of a missionary congregation.

Those two focal points represent the *engaged* and the *distinctive* aspects of the local church. The engaged aspect refers to the way in which, at both the personal and social structures, a church needs to be part of the life of the community in which it is set. The distinctive aspect refers to the way in which the church, again both individuals and the faith community, expresses a 'different way of seeing and living life'.

[2] Matthew, 5:13.

The many different triangles which go to make up the ellipse represent a whole series of different ways of building the church on the basis of its engaged/distinctive nature. A healthy missionary congregation holds together within its life the interplay of being both effectively engaged with the surrounding community and yet also expressing something distinctive within that culture.

It is worth pointing out that the axis of such an ellipse, with these two focal points, highlights some interesting dynamics of local churches (see Figure two below). On a rural/urban axis it is soon evident that rural churches find it easier to be engaged and more difficult to be distinctive. Particularly in the case of Anglican churches, the tendency in the rural community is for the church to be seen as the symbol of the religious and social life of the community. As such it is required to represent all and hold all within its ranks. 'Repent and believe the gospel' does not fit well as a unifying factor in such a situation! However, for urban churches (and the more they are part of large conurbations, the more true this is of them) although they find it easier to be distinctive they often struggle to be properly engaged with the local community.

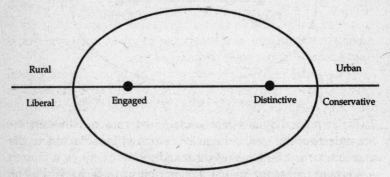

Figure two: the effects of location and tradition on the way the church operates

It is important to note here that in the midst of so much cultural variety in today's society a rural church that is *appropriately engaged and distinctive* will look very different from an urban church that is both engaged and distinctive. Indeed, one appropriately engaged and distinctive rural church will look quite different from another such church. There is no longer simply one way of being church.

> There are many possible forms of church life in modern society and no one form is normative.[3]

The axis can also be used to highlight the distinction between different traditions within the church. Conservative or traditional churches find it easier to be distinctive than engaged, and liberal churches find it easier to be engaged than distinctive.

The essential point is that any church that allows itself to be polarized as belonging to a totally gathered or totally dispersed church style will have lost the necessary creative tension of a missionary congregation which is both engaged and distinctive.

Are they attainable?

The argument here is that the church is set in inherited mode, and that the only way of making progress is to 'abandon ship'. Those who argue for such an approach believe that attempting to 'turn the whole ship round' is too difficult a task. Moreover, the argument is that church culture, that is, the way the church operates, is a severe obstacle to any significant change.

If this is true then the only way is to begin again. There are good reasons for 'starting again', as we shall see in a later chapter. It is certainly the quickest way to bring about change. It also has the value of modelling answers to the wider church. However, we should be reluctant to 'abandon the church as it now is' and simply concentrate on new forms of church life.

Certainly it is true that it will not be possible to shift every church. Some are in terminal decline and need to be allowed, indeed helped, to die with dignity. Others are, for the present at least, blocked – often through the hijacking of power within the

---

[3] 'The Church for Others' (WCC Report), p.83.

existing structures. As one church leader put it, 'We are only two deaths away from revival!'

Yet it is possible to believe that a major shift in focus is possible across the board in the life of the church today. Resistance to change is a real obstacle, but it can be overcome. Moreover, there are a number of factors likely to stimulate the shift to a new way of being church for many 'normal' churches.

Sheer survival is not necessarily the best motivation for change, but it does sometimes work wonders. Indeed the financial losses of the Church Commissioners may well already be acting as a significant catalyst for change, even if it casts the Commissioners in the unlikely role of 'agent of mission'! Perhaps, particularly in scattered rural communities where clergy are ever more thinly spread, the church membership may well rise up to say, 'what are *we* going to do about it?' That one step can bring about a major shift into a church energized by lay vitality after years of passive membership.

The ordination of women may well be another spark that brings new life to existing churches. Their leadership style could be just what the church needs if it is to engage with the current search for meaning and significance. Anecdotal evidence suggests that it is unusual to find a woman leading a church which is not growing. Such churches are often growing in humanity prior to their growing in numbers. It may well be that their different leadership style will help the church to embody the gospel before it attempts to disseminate it. It could make for a more reflective and less frantic church; a church able to build community both in, and beyond its ranks. Like Esther we may well be right to say to such women, 'who knows but that you have come to royal position for such a time as this?' (Esther 4:14), not that such women would see the priesthood in terms of royalty, power or control. Like Deborah, their community building skills may well be the missionary work of the church in the many places where 'natural community' has broken down:

> Village life in Israel ceased, ceased until I, Deborah, arose, arose a mother in Israel.[4]

[4] Judges 5:8.

Sheer relief may well also prove to be a powerful force for change. In due course it will be argued that the primary task of a missionary congregation is to live out the fullness of our humanity opened up for us in Christ. Churches which have been struggling to maintain existing and often outmoded structures and ways of operating may find this such good news that all sorts of sacrifices and costs will be embraced because of the 'joy that is set before us'.

Equally, if such a way of seeing the good news is the way that will communicate itself in today's culture, then there could be a significant resonance with this message in the surrounding community. If, in other words, the search for meaning is at the heart of society's hunger today, then, once a church embraces this option for change, it could well find a people eager to hear. We will only need to see a few such churches emerging before the rest of the church has first its attention, and then its agenda, turned round.

Time may also, in a strange way, be on the side of change. It could well be that the only churches which survive over the next couple of decades are the ones that have embraced the missionary agenda. Those which 'play safe' with the old ways of operating may find themselves disappearing.

Yes, the change to a missionary dynamic is a massive shift. It may well involve nothing less than the conversion of local church communities. However, the time is ripe, and the 'crisis' sufficient to provoke attention. Certainly groups should be released which are incarnating the gospel, but we should not abandon the attempt to turn the whole ship round.

The above argument about missionary congregations not being achievable is based on the judgment that the normal church in inherited mode is too stuck in its ways. Another argument against attempting to turn the whole Church into a 'movement for mission'[5] comes from the students of church history. It is pointed out that the church has always tended to operate in 'pastoral mode', with various para-church organizations being responsible for mission. In the Catholic Church the para-church organizations

[5] Lambeth Pastoral Letter, 7:13, p.327.

take the form of the Religious Orders, such as Jesuits and Franciscans. They are the missionary movements of the Catholic Church. In the Protestant tradition the same missionary work has been expressed through the missionary societies. History, it is argued, suggests that the local church always and only functions in pastoral mode.

This would seem to be reinforced by the history of a denomination such as Methodism. It began as a missionary thrust from within the Anglican Church. It may well have looked like a religious order ('Methodism' refers to the 'method' or rule of life adopted by those involved) emerging within Anglicanism. However, such 'commitment' was so foreign to Anglicanism that this organ transplant (giving the Church of England a 'missionary heart') was just not possible. Rejection set in and the new organ was removed. Moreover, when this new organ became an organization, Method*ism*, a sure and steady shift from mission to pastoral structures set in. Today most Methodists would acknowledge that their church is no more 'missionary' than any other denomination.

Are we then shut up to these competing alternatives, the local church in pastoral mode and the non-local organization in mission mode? There is a way through that this book argues. It is that we are not to abandon the pastoral in the search for the missionary, but rather we are to marry it to the missionary. Equally we need to root the missionary in the pastoral. If we could identify the truth of the gospel in such a way that the pastoral and missionary aspects of the church were both subsumed and expressed within one higher and integrating vision, then we could lay the foundations for a sustainable expression of a mission-orientated pastoral church.

That is how the church seems to have functioned in New Testament times and in the early centuries. Yes, there were mission-structures of which Paul's missionary journeys and the missions of Celtic missionary bishops are two examples. Yet the church which resulted grew to influence, and in time, to evangelize whole cultures – by the quality of their living more than by the quantity of the activity. It is that vision which undergirds the understanding of the church in mission mode advocated here. How such a vision might work in practice, and how it is already emerging, is what the rest of this book will address.

Are they sustainable?

One of the arguments against missionary congregations has been that 'you cannot sustain a missionary congregation; it is like a ring doughnut, there is nothing at the centre.'

This is a valid criticism of some approaches to building missionary congregations. Typical of such approaches is the famous dictum of Archbishop William Temple who said that 'the church is the only organization which exists ("entirely", or did he mean/say "primarily") for the benefit of non-members.' It is another of those slogans which by exaggerating the case ends up undermining it. It results in casualties from 'friendly fire'.

Certainly 'all mission and no play makes Jack (and Jill) a dull church.' If mission is all about 'going out and getting them in', then this is a valid objection. And some 'missionary churches' are like that; they have a recruiting view of evangelism. Such congregations are rather like a shopkeeper who stands outside the shop trying to persuade people to come in. These 'customers' are not, however, being invited in to buy, but rather to help persuade other people to come in who in turn are not being invited to buy but to help persuade other people to come in . . . and so on. All the time, there is actually nothing on the shelves to buy. It is a sales-addicted organization. That is not a healthy model of a missionary congregation, though it is sometimes the picture that people have at the back of their minds.

A healthy missionary congregation is rather a community of people committed to exploring and living the truth of God's revelation in Christ as it touches the whole of their living. As such it may well be a place which is marked by stillness and the ability to reflect on the joys and struggles of life. It is for this reason that, splendid sentiment though it sounds, we cannot actually

subscribe to Emil Bruner's saying that 'the church exists by
mission as fire exists by burning.' Replace the word 'mission' by
'love', and then we are speaking truth. One of the quickest ways
for a church to become a missionary congregation would be for it
to commit itself to live by the two great commandments and to
support each other to live the whole of our lives with that as the
basis. This, however, will produce a quite different church from
one that is focused on the doing of endless 'mission work'. The
latter approach is not a sustainable model.

This false recruiting approach to mission creates a church in
'activist' mode. Such churches are often actually functioning
within the *inherited* mode that has already been explored.
However, as the result of great enthusiasm and heroic effort,
they have managed to stir up enough mission activity to draw
others into the life of the church. It is this approach which
cannot be sustained. Indeed such churches tend to have a high
turnover of members (and leaders) simply because people cannot
sustain that high level of activity and commitment over a long
period. As the Green movement is looking and arguing for an
ecologically sustainable economics, so the Church should be
looking for a joyfully sustainable model of being a missionary
church.

However, and this is the vital point, to define the gospel as
entering into the gift of full humanity, the new creation,[6] as demonstrated and made available in Christ, does two vital things. Not
only does it clothe the gospel for today's culture; it also creates a
life-giving interactive loop between being and doing, between
church life and mission activity.

It is at just this point that the WCC 'The Church for Others'
report was weak, in that it saw the church so much as an instrument of the kingdom, the means of forwarding God's mission in
the world, that it failed to recognize that it is also an end in itself.
Moreover, it also developed too activist a model of church life – the
'sales-addicted' mode identified above. To its credit, it has recog-

[6] 2 Corinthians 5:17.

nized both these weaknesses in its more recent work.[7]

The fact is that a missionary congregation is one which sees its calling as both to be and to tell the good news. It is both a means to an end, the forwarding of God's mission in the world, and a sign of the end, the community of the Age to Come. It is the community whose life consists in the celebration and enjoyment of the liberating wholeness of Jesus Christ. This is a sustainable model, run on the renewable resources of God's grace, empowered by the alternating currents of giving and receiving the gift of the new humanity. On sale in the shop is the staff, and the stuff, of life. The sales line reads:

> Come, all you who are thirsty,
> come to the waters;
> and you who have no money,
> come, buy wine and milk
> without money and without cost.
> Why spend your money on what is not bread,
> and your labour on what does not satisfy?
> Listen, listen to me, and eat what is good,
> and your soul will delight in the richest of fare.
> Give ear and come to me; hear me, that your soul may live.[8]

Truly, there is jam in the centre of this doughnut!

[7] See Gerhard Linn's article 'Towards New Community in Mission', in the *International Review of Mission* . . .
[8] Isaiah 55:1-3.

5

Models of the Emerging Church

In this tumbled present we must build,
for damaged beauty needs a new design.
John Bates, *Damaged beauty needs a new design.*

The best answer to all objections to 'missionary congregations' is to point to churches which are modelling creative new ways of being church. This chapter explores six such portraits. They show a remarkable and rich variety in the life of the church. They are stories that circle the globe.

One thing these churches have in common is that their stories have been written down. This is why they have been chosen. It means that their stories are accessible to all. It also enables a broad, and indeed both ecumenical and global picture, to be built up. Certainly the six stories told here demonstrate that restricting the examples to written stories is no inhibition on the range and variety of such churches; rather the reverse. It was Robert Zend who said, 'People have one thing in common, they are all different.' The same can be said of emerging models of church life. Because of their inner vitality and creativity, and because of their commitment to live the gospel in the particular setting in which they find themselves, they express their life in a great variety of ways.[1]

[1] In part two of Melba Maggay's, *Transforming Society*, the author explores five models which the Church has used in the course of its history to engage in the mission of transforming society. It is helpful to set those models (community, consensus, liberation, compassion, and prophecy) alongside the six stories in this

One particular aspect of the variety of these stories is the different theological traditions they represent. What follows are accounts of churches that draw their insights and spiritual life from the liberal, Catholic, evangelical, and charismatic traditions within the Church. All types of churchmanship are represented. That is good news for the Church, for it means that becoming a church renewed in mission is possible for churches of all types and traditions. However, if that is the good news, the bad, or at least tough, news is that each tradition has needed to go through a deep reworking of its theology in order to become a contemporary church in mission. Indeed this is a crucial characteristic of the emerging church. It is a church that takes its inherited tradition, and renews and reinterprets it for the contemporary setting.

The purpose of these stories is to give us a broad canvas on which to work. Later chapters will give more specific suggestions about the 'how to' developing emerging churches. That is not the primary purpose of this chapter, which is rather to broaden the horizon of our thinking. However, connections with practice and possible lines of action will be made throughout this worldwide tour of missionary congregations.

The Isaiah vision

The title comes from the book of that name written by Raymond Fung, who developed his ideas whilst working at the World Council of Churches Commission on World Mission and Evangelism. It is good to start with something from that source for the whole concept of missionary congregations originated with the World Council of Churches.[2]

In *The Isaiah Vision* Raymond Fung does not give the story of one church engaged in mission, nor is he writing simply out of theory, but rather out of the observation of a pattern that he has seen as he travelled the world in search of such churches.

[2] 'The Church for Others' report (1968), which contains two reports, one European and one North American on The Missionary Structure of the Congregation.

We have consulted and tested the material with evangelists and teachers in many lands, from Central America to the Middle East, from India and South East Asia to the Sudan, from Aotearoa-New Zealand/Australia to North America and Europe.[3]

So here is a model that has been tried and tested and found applicable across the globe. It warrants our careful consideration. It is a disarmingly simple threefold process.

Partnership, worship and discipleship – together these three elements make up this ecumenical evangelistic strategy for the local congregation.[4]

What he has observed, and advocates, is not so much a model or organizational structure for a church engaged in mission, but rather a *mission agenda*. If that agenda or programme is adopted it will have far-reaching effects on the life of the church and its assessment of what is important, and what can be disposed of, in its life.

Dr Fung advocates a partnership approach to local needs with any individual or group, whether voluntary or governmental, who is willing to work on the same agenda. The agenda which he proposes is the one spelt out in Isaiah 60:20-23 which he summarizes in these terms:

The Isaiah vision describes what God wants to see happen in human community. It is a community in which:
– children do not die;
– old people live in dignity;
– people who build houses live in them; and
– those who plant vineyards eat the fruit.[5]

Some have questioned the use of this particular passage. Why not, for example, if one is going to use a passage from Isaiah, use the

[3] Raymond Fung, *The Isaiah Vision*, p.viii.
[4] Ibid., p.3.
[5] Ibid. p.5.

great vision of a new Jubilee from Isaiah 61 which Jesus picked up as the theme of his ministry in his first sermon as recorded in Luke 4:14ff? Raymond Fung's answer is that the passage he has chosen is deliberately 'minimalist in its understanding of human need' and therefore forms a good starting point. By all means move on beyond this vision, he would say, but here is a good starting point, for:

> . . . it is biblical, it makes universal sense, it communicates well, it is easy to contextualize, and it is useful as a measure to assess human behaviour; actions and policies.[6]

Having established that biblical vision, he then proposes a three-fold process of engagement with the community around. The first step is *an invitation to partnership* with others of good will – not least, this means for us in the UK setting, with government social agencies – on the four key aspects of this vision, namely children, the elderly, and housing and work issues. Though in the Third World these issues seem more obvious, they are also major issues in almost every area in our own country. For example, some of the most vicious and motiveless murders recently perpetrated have been done by young people from stable suburban homes 'just for the hell of it'. Such communities have more than their fair share of both broken homes and alcohol and drug abuse. The Isaiah agenda touches even the most stable and respectable areas today. Deep human need and dark human motivation lurk just below the surface of most communities.

Having joined in partnership with others to address human need in the local setting, the second stage is *an invitation to worship*. This can most easily take place as an opportunity to celebrate together what has happened, and to stop and reflect on the journey so far. Celebration is a deep human instinct, and the Church can provide that – pointing, in that context, to the Author and Giver of All-as a focus of reflection and celebration for the wider community. We will return to the centrality of celebration in

6 Ibid., p.5.

due course. Recent surveys indicate that a higher proportion of church members are involved in social action and caring agencies than the rest of the population. Worship may well be the inspiration for such action and the means of sustaining involvement when nothing but setbacks seem to occur.

The third stage is *the invitation to discipleship*. It arises naturally out of a shared partnership with others, and out of moments of celebration and reflection, where the Christian participants have been able to express the resources of faith that sustain and guide them in the work which is being done.

Simplicity is one of the things that shines through *The Isaiah Vision*. It is only fifty-five pages long! That simplicity can be deceptive. Some may well feel 'this is not evangelistic and radical enough'. Yet it only claims to be a starting point – a point at which to start to apply and live out the practical implications of the gospel. It is a tried and tested pattern that has brought focus, renewed energy for mission and the fruit of evangelism into churches across the globe. It does not look well against some of the church growth 'sure fire success models' but it may well be truer to the gospel for that very reason. Those, who like Naaman, are looking for something big and dramatic to do for God[7] may miss the prophetic insights of what he has to say.

In most of the ordinary parishes of this land, such an approach would provide a clear and straightforward *starting point*. By turning its attention to the mission agenda in the community around it[8] a church may well discover many answers to the question about how to be the church in that setting. The adoption of such an agenda could be the beginning of a whole new way of discovering what really matters in the life of the church, and indeed in the whole of life. Especially might this be so if it is done in the context of a parish audit.

[7] 2 Kings 5.

[8] John Reader's, *Local Theology Church and Community in Dialogue* is a valuable English expression and outworking of *The Isaiah Vision*. I recommend that the two books be read together to gain a good perspective.

Open Doors, Open Minds

The next story is both in great continuity with the Isaiah vision and in marked contrast. The continuity arises from the fact that it is the story of one church seeking to address the physical and social needs of people in its own community, and finding that its faith and life and whole understanding of 'church' and 'mission' were evangelized in the process. The contrast is that it is the story of just one church, and that a strongly evangelical one.

The story is of St John's, Boscombe. It is a church set in that most remarkable of contradictions for all who do not know the area, namely an Urban Priority Area in Bournemouth. The church was established over a hundred years ago out of an evangelical reaction to the establishing of another, strongly anglo-catholic church in the area. Ever since that time St John's has had a reputation as a fine evangelical 'preaching shop'.

However, a new vicar, Godfrey Taylor, arriving with a fresh set of eyes, was appointed soon after the church was beginning to face the implication of being set in a UPA area. This was due largely to the fact that the parish had become part of bed-sit land where many of those on social benefit found (all too temporary) housing. Drug and alcohol abuse, poor living conditions, mental health problems and, usually, great loneliness, were all common problems. The church certainly did not reflect that sort of social mix; it was a largely eclectic, middle-class, congregation.

It was this discontinuity between church and community which Godfrey Taylor and the leadership within the church had the courage to face. It resulted initially in a vision to reshape the West End of the church as a place which could be open every day of the week as a coffee bar where people could come and find friendship and help. What began as the work of reordering the church building (Open Doors) led, however, to a deep restructuring of the spirituality and lifestyle of the church and its members (Open Minds). It involved the shift from;

'the mentality of the "gathered" church – focused on the

membership rather than the parish – which had shaped the congregation's thinking for many years . . ."[9]

It also involved the shift from a 'preaching shop' mentality and way of operating. This meant a profound change in how people saw and lived the gospel and were the church.

> The immediate action demanded of us was not just to go on declaring his truth but to start in a new way demonstrating his love . . .The phrase that kept appearing in sermons and prayer meetings was 'availability-evangelism'. The first stage was to say to the people of the area. 'We are here and in Christ's name we care about you.'[10]

It is a moving story of how a church was deeply reworked in its whole perception of how it saw God, the gospel, the world and the Church – and then went on to live out the implications of that shift in perceptions. It is told with great honesty and with a continued sense of journey. It points us both to the need for churches of every tradition to be renewed and to face the cost that such changes involve. Yet, above all, it is a story of the striking fruit that is produced under such pressure. Of all the models of an emerging missionary way of being church recorded in this chapter, this is the story that points most clearly to the way in which there needs to be a conversion of the whole church community if the Church is to be renewed in mission. A willingness to face a change at the core of our understanding of ourselves, God, the faith and the whole of life is essential. It is also life-giving, as this story testifies.

Ecclesiogenesis[11]

The title of this book is enough to frighten off many people, though like Raymond Fung's book, this seminal work is well

---

[9] Derek Baldwin, *Open Doors Open Minds*, p.46.

[10] Ibid., p.87.

[11] Leonardo Boff, *Ecclesiogenesis: The Base Communities Reinvent the Church* (Maryknoll, NY: Orbis Books 1986).

under one hundred pages long. Like Raymond Fung's book it is about many churches rather than one. Written by a leading Roman Catholic Liberation theologian, Leonardo Boff, it is the theoretical basis for a remarkable manifestation of a new way of being church which has come into being in South America over the past few decades. Called 'base communities', they represent a fundamentally new way of being the church.

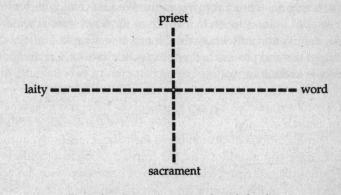

Figure three: Base communities and parish churches.

Base communities, of which there are about eighty thousand in South America, are lay-led groups of people at the 'base' of society (hence their name.) They are communities of poor, marginalized, oppressed people, banding together in the name and presence of Christ to support one another in the midst of a life of deprivation and injustice.

Whereas the typical parish is structured, as Boff points out, on a vertical axis of 'Priest and sacrament', the base communities are built on the horizontal axis of laity and the word. A vital aspect of base communities is that they are *communities*. Indeed there is much about them which draws inspiration from the Exodus, the journey of an oppressed people discovering God and freedom as they live by a different set of values. Worship, fellowship and mission belong together and take part as one. They are a form of extended family and work very much at the physical survival focus of most people's lives. They share such work and resources and skill as they have between them. Usually about twenty to thirty people come together in each base community. They are linked to the parish structure although their relationship with the institutional church has not been without its strains.

Base communities exhibit a whole-life framework of reference and an openness to God in every aspect of their living, not just in the 'church agenda'. Direct copying in the West has met with limited success, but there is much to learn from them not least in areas of social deprivation and where the Church is seeking to confront the principalities and powers in the surrounding culture. Certainly our society is looking for ways of being community, of belonging, that may well be able to draw inspiration from this movement.

The problem of copying any model of the new emerging way of being church is fraught with dangers. Part of the message of these new manifestations of church life is their sheer creativity. In relation to base communities and the transfer of their insights to a Western setting, the problem seems to be connected with the very different feel of the cultures in which the churches are set. Both, from a biblical perspective, are living in a hostile culture. The problem in the West is that consumerism and the 'culture of contentment' are attractive and seductive, whilst in South America the Church in these communities is facing deprivation, corruption and injustice day after day. It remains to be seen, for example, if a whole new way of being church (or maybe a home group) might not emerge if a group of Christians were to take seriously the implications of confronting the destructive forces of a consumer society, and of *finding a way of living prophetically in that context*.

> Might it take us greater courage to resist in word and action the idolatry of consumerism than it has taken us to resist the 'evil empire' of the communist world?[12]

To take a book such as John Kavanaugh's *Still Following Christ in a*

[12] John Kavanaugh, *Still Following Christ in a Consumer Society*, p.166.

Consumer Society, perhaps together with Walter Brueggemann's *The Prophetic Imagination*, and take two years to study them, relate them to life and develop a shared 'rule of life' (or rather a 'way of life') designed to enable each person to live prophetically in our seductive context, would be a major contribution to the discovery of how the church is to be the church in Western consumerist culture today.

The Blessing

We move now from the world of radical Catholic Liberation theology as expressed in South America, to conservative evangelical/charismatic church life in North America. The story of this expression of an emerging new way of being church is called simply *The Blessing*. It is not in fact the story either of one church or a group or pattern of churches. However, it is about how people are handling the whole of life from a Christian perspective. The many stories contained in the book emerged naturally out of churches which have embraced the ideas set out by the authors. *The Blessing* is written by two authors whose primary work is in a Christian counselling organization called Family Heritage Ministries, based in Phoenix, Arizona.

The book is basically an exploration and application of the giving of a blessing as that practice unfolds in both the Old Testament and the New Testament. From the charismatic/evangelical perspective from which they view the subject, the authors identify five marks of blessings in Scripture. Their key definition is:

> A family blessing begins with *meaningful touching*. It continues with a *spoken message* of *high value*, a message that pictures *a special future* for the individual being blessed, and one that is based on an *active commitment to see the blessing come to pass*.[13]

---

[13] Gary Smalley and John Trent, *The Blessing*, p.24. My italics added to highlight the five aspects.

The book then unpacks each of the five elements, illustrating what they say with a wealth of personal stories of people who have discovered the truths in their experience of life. They include plenty of stories of people who have encountered such blessing within the local church, as well as many who have taken such principles and applied them to the whole of life. As the authors say:

> A church that is committed to applying the principles of the blessing can make a tremendous impact on the unsaved. Once church members learn about this concept and experience it within the church, they can begin to transport it outside the church walls. Monday through Saturday they can provide the elements of God's blessing to a non-Christian society desperately in search of genuine security and acceptance.[11]

Which is why the book is included in this section of models of new ways of being church, for what the authors are describing is how a church can enter into its calling, as a community, to be a priesthood of believers. That New Testament concept has lain dormant for many years, smothered by the clericalism of the Church of the Middle Ages. The Reformers sought to reassert the priority and primary nature of the 'priesthood of all believers'. However, their efforts suffered from two major weaknesses. First, it was more about taking priesthood off clergy than giving it to laity. Second, it was an individualistic reading of the New Testament through which what was really being taught was the 'priesthood of each believer', even 'every man as his own pope'. The biblical concept points rather to a community calling – 'We together, as the local church, form one priesthood, the priesthood that arises out of our being a community, a priestly community.' That is the sense in which the term is used in the New Testament.

Moreover, this awareness of the charismatic dimension of biblical blessing is being applied in some of the strongest growing churches from Pentecostal to Catholic across the globe.

11 Ibid., p. 193.

In such churches the members gather together in small cell groups to support one another. This is no introverted 'holy huddle', but rather the 'equipping of the saints for the work of ministry'. In one such church (a Catholic church in Italy), the members of the cell group come together each week to support each other in the outworking of their discipleship during the coming week. One particular question is asked, namely, 'Who do you find most difficult to work/be with at the present time?' On the principle of praying for our enemies, and 'blessing those who persecute us', the members of the group are then called upon to pray for their 'enemy', to be alert to any way that God might want them to be a blessing to such people in the coming week. This understanding of blessing incorporates the call to bless others by serving them.

The authors of *The Blessing*, coming as they do from the evangelical/charismatic tradition, would find that the words of our next author, Bishop John Robinson, a radical/Catholic, were words they could gladly assent to, when he writes:

> One of the truly revolutionary claims and characteristics of the early Church was what is called the 'common ownership', the koinonia, of Holy Spirit. Hitherto the 'holy' had been defined as that which was not 'common' – and the 'holy' was the sphere of the priest. With the communalization of the holy went the communalization of the priesthood.[15]

This pattern of blessing others in the whole of life is a good model for a number of important characteristics of the church renewed in mission. It shows how crucial an all-embracing spirituality (in this case '*blessing*') is for the energizing of a local church. It also shows how what is learned *in* church needs to be taken *out* from church and connected with the whole of life. It also models an integrated way of being human and being church. Both involve the courage to listen to God and act on what he is telling us. It is a model which many churches could adopt, adapt and apply to the way that they

[15] John Robinson, *On Being the Church in the World*, p.76.

work. To do so, although it would take a couple of years to allow it to flow through the lifeblood of a whole church, would be to reorientate the church around its missionary calling. It would be likely to bring into being a renewal which sprang out of the roots of the church's spirituality. Many existing activities would look different in the light of such a focus. It could well result in a clear recognition of the need for change in the inherited ways of being church.

Liturgy come to life

We now return to England, albeit to England in the later 1960s and to the work of Bishop John Robinson when he was Dean of Clare College, Cambridge.

This model of a missionary congregation is a striking story. It has the wonderful advantage of being quite unrepeatable! That may seem a strange form of praise. However, the fact is that missionary congregations are creative and original works of God and are not reproduced by copying. We can frequently learn from them but we can rarely copy them. The fact that this 'church' is set in an all-male residential college in one of the two top universities in England, in which the 'parish' (namely the non-chapel-going majority) consisted of young men of whom between eighty and ninety per cent were baptized and confirmed Anglicans, is no disadvantage. What can be learned is how the issue of being church was addressed by this original practitioner of theology.

The story is essentially one of making the Eucharist a living reality to all who participated in it. This was done by majoring on the fourfold action of the Eucharist, namely the action of Jesus in *taking*, *blessing*, *breaking* and *giving* the bread and wine to his disciples. This fourfold action was not only drawn out as the essential movement of the service, but as the essential pattern of God's handling of the life of the believer; for he takes us, blesses us, breaks us and gives us to his world. Hence John Robinson's concern with the Eucharist:

> I am interested in liturgy only as the clue to the transfiguration of life by the kingdom of God.[16]

The book is the story of how each part of the Eucharist was taken and brought to life and brought into relationship with the whole of life. Few who participated in such services could fail to have been made aware of the sacredness of the whole of life or of the intricate interweaving of worship and work which constitutes the very nature of 'living eucharistically'. As Robinson puts it:

> Now if the Eucharist is thus the heart and hub of social action, the point where this world is taken and consecrated, broken and restored to God and his kingdom, and where the Church itself is renewed as the agent of the Christian revolution, then we must learn again what the early Church meant when it spoke so naturally of 'doing the Eucharist'.[17]

Other authors, independently of John Robinson, have picked up the same theme. Notably Henri Nouwen in his book *The Life of the Beloved*, who uses the fourfold action to develop a contemporary eucharistic spirituality. Michael Crosby, in his book on the Lord's Prayer, entitled *Thy Will Be Done* (subtitled *Praying the Our Father As Subversive Activity*), deals with the outworking of the fourfold action in Chapter seven, on 'Give us this day our daily bread'. In it, echoing the words of John Robinson, he says:

> Our ritual must be at the centre of our daily living. It cannot be at life's periphery . . . In other words, only by carrying into the liturgy our deeds of justice and from the liturgy our commitment to be its ministers in the world will our prayer be heard, our prayer in which we ask that our sacrifice be acceptable to God, our almighty Father.[18]

The significance of this story is that the integration of liturgy and life is at the heart of what energizes a missionary congregation.

[16] John Robinson, *Liturgy Come to Life*, p.xi.
[17] Ibid., p.16.
[18] Michael Crosby, *Thy Will Be Done*, p.134/5.

Such a congregation is a community of faith which has redis-covered worship as the renewal of the church's awareness of God, renewal of the worshippers' identity as children and servants of God and also the place where the whole of life is given meaning and purpose through the knowledge of God. Here is a model of how the church, through a renewal of its Eucharistic life and spirituality, can engage in mission.

Local Theology

We move now to rural Shropshire, perhaps not the place we would most naturally look for a model of the emerging church. Yet here, through John Reader's book of the above title, we find someone wrestling with and applying many of the ideas expressed in this book.

It is the story of a church which sought to apply its theology to how it expressed its life and engaged in mission. It has done so in a thoroughly post-modern way. Rather than imposing some theo-logical framework ('grand narrative') on the church and com-munity, the church sought to address the issues of the local community – and take time to reflect theologically on the issues. It did so by tackling several projects.

The key group it worked with, and here is a further unlikely source of inspiration for the church in mission mode, was the Local History Group. This was not a church group, but became the focus of community action in the area. The 'work' it took on were issued of housing and the environment. The book tells the story of how these projects emerged and of the struggles involved in getting the projects established. Those struggles were primarily about issues of power which caused them to reflect on power from a Christian perspective. This in turn raised issues about the nature of commu-nity and a Christian perspective on the divide between the 'rock' of capitalist individuals and the 'hard place' of socialist totalitarian-ism. In tackling an environmental project, power issues again surfaced, as did questions about a Christian approach to 'Green issues'. A specific local project was allowed to raise questions for the church, which as with the other project, led them to an under-standing that went well beyond the specific project.

In approaching these issues a deliberate choice was made to work from the specific and practical towards a fuller understanding of the issues. In other words it was a practice-to-theory journey (though it was more a dialogue than a two-stage operation), rather than the more normal (and now dated) 'Enlightenment' approach of 'theory-to-practice'. A similar conscious choice was made to approach issues from a spirituality perspective rather than a doctrinal one. As John Reader puts it:

> Attempts to rework and reinterpret Christian doctrine are of interest only to a few, even within the church. Most people require more practical and immediate response, and those on the fringes of, or beyond, Christianity seem more likely to find common ground in the broad area of spirituality.[19]

The whole approach to this work is full of rich insights and great relevance to the church in its present setting. This is one of the most thoroughly worked through responses to our present setting. It incorporates the principle of continual dialogue between 'gospel and culture' which forms the basis of what I have to say about how the shift from inherited to emerging mode can be brought about. John Reader's contribution to this whole shift will be drawn on repeatedly in the last section of this book.

Conclusion

This exploration of different modes of the emerging church has taken us not only across all the divides of church tradition but around the world. We began with Raymond Fung whose roots are in the Far East and South-East Asia. Stopping off in Bournemouth, we moved on then to South America and then, via North America, we returned to the UK in the last two models, going first to Cambridge and then on to South-West Shropshire.

[19] John Reader, *Local Theology*, p.126.

In the coming chapters we shall return to these themes and to the varied stories told in this chapter. They have been told here both as one of the best answers to the objections previously considered and also as examples of the principles of the emerging model of church. They have also been told by way of preparation for the next stage of our journey – the identification of common themes and characteristics in the emerging missionary nature of the church.

6

Marks of the Emerging Church

Jesus did not write a book, but formed a community.

Lesslie Newbigin,
The Gospel in a Pluralist Society, p.227.

You yourselves are our letter . . . known and read by
everybody . . . a letter from Christ written not with ink
but with the Spirit of the living God, not on tablets of
stone but on tablets of human hearts.

2 Corinthians 3:2-3.

So far we have identified the need for the church to change its
ways. But how? That is the question which cries out for an answer
and the one which will be addressed in this chapter. The danger
here is that we approach the question with a blueprint mentality;
that is, with an expectation that there is one 'successful' way to be
an emerging missionary church which, if everyone were to adopt,
would result in all our problems being solved. It simply is not true
that there is only one way of being a church renewed in mission.
Indeed, the opposite is nearer the truth. One of the weaknesses of
the inherited mode of church life is that it has functioned as if there
were only one way of doing things. A church in mission mode
will be marked rather by uniqueness and diversity. The attitude,
although rarely expressed in words, but often lurking only just
below the surface of discussions on this subject, that there is only
one way of being church, is unhelpfully simplistic. As the philos-
opher H.L Mencken put it:

For every difficult and complex question there is an answer
that is simple, easily understood – and wrong!

Signposts

If we cannot settle for just one way of being church, and if we
cannot copy (in entirety) any one way of being church, then what
help is there? Have we been led along a path of seeing the vital role
of the church as the 'primary agent of mission', in having some
understanding of culture as the context for mission, and seeing
how history has cornered the church into a position from which it
must break out, only to discover that the moment we come out of
the woods we find ourselves hanging over a precipice of total,
unrepeatable, creativity? Has the journey led us thus far only to
abandon us to our fate? The fact that this book is not yet half way
through suggests that all is not yet lost!

There is a way. But it is just that – a Way. A path with a number of
signposts and turning points, places of costly decision which must
be addressed and passed. Churches which have taken this journey
have come across these places and found them to be not only crisis
points but also points of creativity, growth, adventure and blessing. So there is a way, but it is not at the level of technique but
rather of turning points and testimony.

Not least is this so since no church can be defined as having
'arrived' as a missionary congregation; for a church renewed in
mission is one that is making a journey. That journey, or mission, it
to be listening continually to the directions inspired of the Spirit
that are emerging from the midst of its life, as well as, seemingly,
from out of the blue.

Four words encapsulate the nature of the church in mission
mode. It is a church *incarnate* in a particular context and setting
(not necessarily a geographical one), and one which is *integrating*
its whole life, rather than dividing itself and its life into neat and
separate compartments. It is also a church which is energized by
a vital *spirituality*. It is also marked by an awareness of being a

community. These emerging churches have discovered their life renewed around an openness to God, to each other and to the world. We turn now to consider these four aspects in greater detail.

The incarnate church

The first mark, or marker, for a missionary congregation is that it is *in* a particular setting, and indeed is part of that context. For the *Isaiah vision*, and for *Base communities* that is the starting point for such congregations existing. For the two English examples in the previous chapter (*Open Doors, Open Minds* and *Liturgy For Life*), their incarnate nature was rather different. It was the urge to become engaged with the local context which gave these two churches not only their sense of mission but their identity. In other words, a missionary congregation may begin as a group of Christians involved in a particular context, or it may be a group who feel impelled by the Spirit to become involved. Either way they share in the nature of Christ's work by becoming incarnate in a particular situation.

Vital to the expression of such a church is the fact that it has a *whole-life focus* rather than just, or primarily, a *church-life* one. The latter characteristic of the church in inherited mode is often a reflection of a deeper sense of retreat from life. Such a whole-life focus comes from a theological conviction about the nature of the mission in which the church is involved.

David Bosch, in his foundational work on the paradigm shifts in the theology of mission[1] identifies a number of elements of an emerging ecumenical missionary paradigm. A key characteristic in this emerging understanding of mission is what he calls 'mission as *missio dei*' (*God's mission*). This is the understanding that God's mission is already up and running, and both prior to and bigger than the church. Mission is not basically something that the church does – to forward God's cause on earth. Rather it is

[1] David Bosch, *Transforming Mission.*

something that God is doing, and in which the church is called to participate. Good recent models of this are the roles which the churches fulfilled in the liberation of many parts of Eastern Europe from the scourge of totalitarianism and which were played by the churches in the liberation of South Africa from apartheid.

From this framework of reference the mission of God is seen in cosmic dimensions first. It concerns the sustaining of all creation until the completion at the End of Time,[2] the gathering up of everything into Christ[3] and the bringing into being of a new heaven and a new earth.[4] This work of completion will include the nations bringing their wealth (material and cultural) into the purposes of God.[5] But it will, and in Christ does, touch the life of all who are open to God's grace, making them part of his new creation[6] and of the new humanity opened up for all through the life, death and resurrection of Christ, the second Adam.[7] It is within this framework that all of human life, and indeed the cosmos and the environment, are brought within the mission purposes of God. This is why emerging churches have an incarnate lifestyle, for they see themselves as called to participate in Christ's continuing incarnate mission towards the ultimate purposes of God for his world.

Another way of saying this is that the emerging church takes its agenda and identity as much from the future as the past. It is looking forward to God's purposes being worked out in the whole of creation.

> Christians live in the space between the unity that is already God's gift in Christ's victory through the Spirit, and that total communion which will be in Christ when the whole creation knows fulfilment.[8]

[2] Romans 8:18-27.
[3] Ephesians 1:8-9, Colossians 1:15-16, 1 Corinthians 15:25-29.
[4] Revelation 21 and 22.
[5] Revelation 21:24.
[6] 2 Corinthians 5:17.
[7] Romans 5:12-21, 1 Corinthians 15:21-24.
[8] Robin Greenwood, *Transforming Priesthood*, p.113.

Sadly, 'eschatology', which is meant to be the study of 'what Christians think about the Last Things', has all too often been better defined as 'the last things Christians think about'. Yet if the emerging church is a journey of faith, it is important to know its destination. The church which is in the vanguard of the changes in society will need to be a church enlivened by hope. The doctrine of eschatology, and the virtue of hope, are part of what will be essential equipment for such a journey.

Integrating

A second characteristic of emerging churches is that they are finding ways of integrating the various, and all too easily fragmented, aspects of life. This disintegration of life is a major characteristic of modern culture. It has been fuelled by a number of forces.

Science has, by its very method, been concerned to take things apart and find out how they work – including, with consequences we could never have imagined, the splitting of the atom. Wonderful for finding out the mechanisms of life in all its forms, such an approach has left humanity hungering for wholeness. Not surprisingly, this is one of the major marks of what is called 'postmodernism'. Whereas our exploration of the universe has been based on taking things apart ('the whole is best understood by detailed analysis of each part'), modern culture is shifting towards this hunger for wholeness ('the whole is greater than the sum of the parts'). Churches functioning in emerging mode, quite possibly not always consciously, are instinctively seeking to find ways of expressing faith which makes sense of the whole of life. In this connection it is noteworthy that the number of resources designed to help church members to relate their faith to life is growing significantly. They represent a valuable resource for the church.[9]

From two profoundly different settings this work of integration is a key characteristic. For example, despite the amazing contrasts

[9] See, for example, *Monday Matters* (Board of Education), *Sunday/Monday* (CPAS), *Faith in Life, To Live and Work* (MU).

of the setting of the work of John Robinson in Cambridge (*Liturgy Come to Life*), and of base communities in South America, those two stories both reflect the fruit of a struggle to connect faith to the whole of life. The same principle is at work not only in all of the other stories told in the previous chapter, but also of the untold stories of many emerging missionary churches in the UK today.

Spirituality

The key factor in the integration of the emerging missionary dynamic of the church is the spirituality which animates the whole operation. Far from the 'inner apartheid' of which Richard Foster speaks, this is a spirituality that makes connections with faith in God and the wholeness of life.

The story of *Open Doors, Open Minds* is of a church being both true to its faith inheritance and yet allowing the inherited expression of that faith to be profoundly reworked and enriched by its experience of life and its grappling with the issues raised by its mission. *The Blessing* is the story of individuals and groups who ordered the whole of their living around the call to be the priesthood of all believers. *Liturgy Come to Life* tells how the fourfold action of the Eucharist was used to develop a spirituality which made sense of all life, and of the church's involvement with the surrounding community. So too for base communities, it is the spiritual life which is the hidden source of vitality for such communities.

> We live out the gift of faith, hope, and charity that makes us disciples of the Lord. This experience is our well.[10]

It is out of reflection on this aspect of missionary congregations that the following framework has emerged. The usual view of the church can be expressed by three interlocking circles which illustrate the areas of *worship* (how we relate to God), *community* (by

---

[10] Gustavo Gutierrez, *We Drink From Our Own Wells: the Spiritual Journey of a People* is one of the best articulations of liberation spirituality as the source of liberation theology.

which is meant the 'faith community', and how we handle relationships within the life of the church), and *mission* (how we engage with the surrounding culture). Important though each of these elements is, there is a crucial area of overlap between all three at the centre of the diagram. It is this area that makes the difference. It is the heart of the church's life, namely its *spirituality*. By 'spirituality', is meant *'our understanding and experience of how encounter with God takes place and how such an encounter is sustained.'*

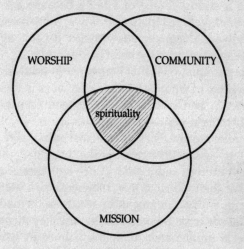

Figure four: the dynamic of spirituality in the local church.

The state of this 'heart' is the crucial factor in the effectiveness of any local church. It is this which explains why two churches which outwardly seem so similar can have such different expressions of life. One shares its faith, is growing, gives generously, pays its quota and exudes a sense of inner vitality expressed in an outer-directed mentality. The other is numerically static at best, complains about the quota, seems lifeless and is often turned in on itself. The difference has to do with spirituality. This is the heart that pumps life into all that takes place. This being so, the task must be to help churches develop their spiritual life so as to enable them to express it through their worship, community and mission.[11]

Churches can fail at several points in this process. Some simply do not have a spirituality. The church is a hive of activity, but essentially a hollow shell. There is nothing at the heart. Some have a spirituality, but because it is not clear or spelt out, it is very difficult for anyone to buy into the underlying ('incipient'?) vitality of the place. Yet others have a spirituality which is clear, but does not function as a strong source of vitality because the church has inherited, or developed patterns of worship, community and mission that are unconnected with (or do not appropriately express) the spirituality at the heart of the church.

Too often the situation is that worship is in gridlock, fellowship is a tangled skein of wool rather than a network of loving relationships, mission is seen as the work of a few enthusiasts each cutting across each other's efforts, and spirituality is simply a puzzle. However, there are churches with a clear spirituality that is well expressed in, and reinforced by, the way they handle their worship, community and mission. Such churches are missionary in nature. We shall return to this framework as a useful model in facilitating the shift of congregations into mission mode.

Again it needs to be pointed out that this key theme of spirituality connects immediately with the culture in which we live which, not least through the New Age movement, is much more alive to the spiritual dimension of life. It is hardly surprising that a church, appropriately engaged with modern society's search for meaning and significance, will pick up on this theme. Indeed, it may be that one of the reasons that earlier attempts at building a missionary dynamic into the local church (especially through *The*

[11] Working quite independently, John Cole, author of the helpful workbook *How To Be a Local Church*, develops a similar model. Based on the gift of *koinonia* as the core of the Christian faith, his three circles are identified as *communion* with God, *community* with one another, and *communication* with the world. In order to avoid any appearance of 'sealed unit spirituality' he did not identify the central triangle as having any existence other than in relation to the respective elements. I commend his workbook.

Church for Others report), may, in the strongly secularized sixties' culture, have lacked access to appropriate and viable spirituality with which such a project might have been energized.

Community

A final common factor in the nature of emerging missionary congregations is the dynamic of community. Relationships in organizations function within role responsibilities and tend to minimize the personal element. In the church this is further constrained by a veneer of 'niceness' and respectability which inhibits the vitality of the church in inherited mode. Churches in emerging mode seem, by contrast, to have been able to harness the positive side of both teamwork and personal vulnerability. In such churches the value of each person for his or her own sake, and human gifting, are blended with an openness to human frailty and limitation.

It is this expression of community which is probably the key element in the evangelistic fruitfulness of such churches, for the visitor or person whose life in any way makes contact with the group discovers that they have stumbled on a very normal group of fallible human beings who yet have developed a most attractive and sustained network of loving relationships.

It is noteworthy that here again, as with the other key factors in the nature of these emerging churches, this is a characteristic which resonates strongly with the hunger of contemporary culture. As Scott Peck puts it:

> We are desperately in need of a new ethic of 'soft individualism', an understanding of individualism which teaches that we cannot be truly ourselves until we are able to share freely the things we most have in common: our weakness, our incompleteness, our imperfection, our inadequacy, our sins, our lack of wholeness and self-sufficiency . . . It is a kind of softness that allows those necessary barriers, or outlines, of our individual selves to be like permeable membranes,

permitting ourselves to seep out and the selves of others to seep in.[12]

The power of Christian community resides in the transparency of its mixture of transcendence and imminence. Transcendence is experienced because true community points to the Trinity of Divine community, the core nature of the whole of reality. Imminence is expressed because it is in the intimacy of personal relationships that love is encountered. There is, as poets, song-writers (and, in today's culture, the advertisers) know all too well, nothing that speaks so universal a language as love itself. 'See how these Christians love one another' is as powerful a magnet today as when it was first said nearly two thousand years ago. It lies at the heart of what it means both to be human and to be church.

It is here that the primary model of the emerging church may be glimpsed. It will involve a shift from the perception of:

$$\text{church} = \text{building} + \text{priest} + \text{stipend}$$
$$\text{to}$$
$$\text{church} = \text{community} + \text{faith} + \text{action}$$

Interestingly the common usage of the word 'church' relates to the first formula. So 'going to church' means going to a building; and 'going into the church' refers to ordination. There is no equivalent use of the word church which links with the New Testament sense of 'community of faith' – yet!

Defining characteristics

We are now in a position to compare the marks of the emerging missionary nature of the church with the characteristics, identified in Chapter two, of the inherited way of being church. In this way we can see the contrast more clearly.

As far as the *structure* of the emerging church is concerned it is *light and flexible*. This is partly due to the fact that many

[12] M. Scott Peck, *The Different Drum*, p.58, Chapter five 'Stages of Community-making' is a classic outline of the four stages of community building.

organizations and ways of operating in today's culture are like that; it is also because what is primary in such a church is not the inherited structure, but rather the goal and purpose of the church. Once purpose is discerned then structures are shaped to facilitate that purpose. The way the church operates, in other words, is not an end in itself, but rather a means to an end.

In this connection it is interesting to observe what is taking place in modern society in general and the business world in particular. Alvin Tofler, whose best-known work is *Future Shock*, says in another of his books, *The Third Wave*, that the emerging society will be structured not around aristocracy or meritocracy or democracy but around what he calls 'ad-hoc-cracy': that is by great flexibility to meet the present situation. Tom Peters, the business guru, in one of his recent books called significantly *Liberation Management*, speaks of chaos structures for a chaos culture. He is making the same point.

Such a simplified approach suits the church's internal and external situation well. In so many areas, financially, in membership and as far as clergy are concerned, the church is constrained by lack of resources to keep the inherited structures going. One of the results is exhaustion of clergy and church members.[13] It also suits the external situation because the younger generations are certainly 'not into institutions'. They may well give themselves devotedly to the work of the kingdom, to relationships, to issues of justice and compassion, but they have little interest in maintaining institutions. The conscious commitment to simplify, rather than elaborate, may be just what the Spirit is saying to the church today.

> I plead guilty to the charge of 'terrible simplification'. It could be, though, that a certain kind of simplification is long overdue in the business of theologizing . . . many new intellectual departures have become possible only after the luxuriant complexities accumulated before them have once more been reduced to surveyable simplicity.[14]

[13] John Sanford, *Ministry Burnout*, and Marjory Foyle, *Honourably Wounded*.
[14] Peter Berger, *A Rumour of Angels*, p.117.

Leadership is a strong element in the development of emerging churches. Perhaps this is so not least because new ventures often need visionaries to get them launched. We are certainly not talking about the abandonment or rejection of leadership. Indeed one of the criticisms of much training for the ordained ministry is that it does not equip clergy to lead. However, the *leadership style* clearly evident in emerging churches is one that is empowering rather than disabling. *Collaborative* is its key characteristic.

Nothing further needs to be added about the difference in *focus* of the emerging church as marked by a *whole-life* orientation since this has already been spelt out as arguably the key characteristic of a church renewed in mission.

Emerging churches are further characterized in their *form* by being more of a *community* than an organization. No community, of course, can function without structure and organization. However, in emerging churches this is secondary to, and the servant of, a communal way of operation. An organization tends towards a mechanical view of reality, including relationships. It treats people as units of production ('ministry' is the church word for that) and as units of consumption ('worshippers'). It sets up structures to get the most out of these units. It rarely has time for those who are not functioning efficiently as producers or consumers. A community, however, values people for themselves. It also tends to give highest honour to the weak.[15] Communities are orientated more around quality and worth and relationships, whilst organizations are focused on achieving. Emerging churches certainly seem to be 'very productive' although this is not their focus. The 'productivity' is the fruit of the existence of a network of loving relationships and a leadership style which affirms the worth, and draws out the gifts, of every member.

In emerging churches the pastoral goal goes beyond the goal of giving comfort and keeping people happy. Although to describe those marks as characteristic of all churches functioning in the inherited or maintenance mode does them an injustice, yet it has to

" 1 Corinthians 12.23.

be acknowledged that a church committed to keeping itself going will instinctively seek to keep and make people happy. 'Helping people to enjoy the ride', as more than one clergyman has described his role. When the church is being renewed in mission, the pastoral goals shift, sometimes imperceptibly, towards an 'equipping for life' focus and towards an unspoken assumption that personal growth and development are essential 'for life and godliness'[16] in other words a shift towards being *holy*.

The emerging mode of church life is *expressed* in a great *variety* of ways, as the previous chapter clearly demonstrated. This is partly the result of their being purpose orientated. It is the purpose that is the constant, the structures and form are subservient to that goal. So, for example, in the inherited mode of church life the approach to one specific issue, namely the shortage of leaders for uniformed organizations, is likely to be 'We have always had uniformed organization for young people in this church; how can we recruit leaders to keep them going?' In the emerging church, the perspective is much more likely to be 'What are we trying to achieve by our uniformed organizations; are they the best way to achieve this goal; are there other ways?' No overall judgment is being made about the value of uniformed organizations by this illustration. Indeed it is to be expected that different emerging churches will come up with widely differing responses to their appropriateness. This variety is also the fruit of the church harnessing the variety of gifts of its members. It also can be expected because of the variety of ways of relating in our present culture. If the church is to live in and communicate to a society which is now made up of a mosaic of cultures, it should have a mosaic of ways of expressing its life in that community.

Finally, and perhaps most importantly, the emerging church looks to the *future* for its *orientation* and source of inspiration. Not that it ignores the past. Rather it uses the future to shape its reworking of the past. The emerging church draws on the inherited riches of the past to sustain its life in the present as it lives by the values of the Age to Come.

[16] 2 Peter: 3-4.

The New Testament is consistent in describing the times in which we live as the End Times and Last Days. This does not mean primarily that chronologically the clock is almost at midnight, but rather that the character of the times in which the church lives is shaped by the End. Today's culture is in particular need of beginning at the End. Much of the violence in the youth culture stems from a lack of purpose, significance, meaning and hope among young people today. For we live without hope, direction or purpose. The End Times point us to purpose, to the *gathering up* of all things in Christ: *creation, culture* (the nations bringing their wealth before the Lamb), *history, humanity* and the *church* (as the Bride of the True Humanity and second Adam).

The Christian community is to order its life around the values of the Age to Come. It is a community which celebrates, demonstrates and thereby proclaims the gathering up of all creation into the purposes of God revealed in Christ. It is this vision of the End, and thus of what is of lasting importance, incarnate in human experience, through the word of the kingdom, which expresses the Presence of the Future and equips the church to participate in God's mission in the world to redeem the whole creation.

> I would want to challenge the implication that religion cannot be future-orientated ... Christianity has the symbol of the kingdom of God to keep our eyes firmly fixed on the future.[17]

Such a challenge calls the church to move out of the guard's van, where we have been for too long, looking back over the distant and disappearing peaks we have passed (or desperately clutching the brake to slow down the pace of change at every point). We are to get out of the guard's van, recover our nerve, and rediscover our true role in the vanguard of society; shaping the new world order in and after the likeness of Christ. Not now, of course, by means of

[17] John Reader, *Local Theology*, p.134/5. See also Robin Greenwood, *Transforming Priesthood*, Chapter five 'Church: a sign of hope in the world'.

imperial imposition, but rather through incarnate exposition – both of our words and our lives.

Reflection for action

It can be a helpful exercise for a church (and particularly a PCC) to consider where they are in relation to each aspect identified. There is a spectrum of expression for each of them, hence the scale of 1 to 9 underneath each characteristic in Figure five.

Aspect	Inherited					Emerging			
Structure	**fixed/heavy**					**light/flexible**			
	1	2	3	4	5	6	7	8	9
leadership	**clerical/control**					**collaborative/creative**			
	1	2	3	4	5	6	7	8	9
focus	**church-life**					**whole-life**			
	1	2	3	4	5	6	7	8	9
form	**organization**					**community**			
	1	2	3	4	5	6	7	8	9
pastoral goal	**happy**					**holy**			
	1	2	3	4	5	6	7	8	9
expression	**single**					**diverse**			
	1	2	3	4	5	6	7	8	9
orientation	**past**					**future**			
	1	2	3	4	5	6	7	8	9

Figure five: inherited/emerging model spectrum.

When doing such an exercise it is helpful not only to give a score, but also to make a note (to the left of the score) of evidence of the inherited pattern, and (to the right of the score) of any evidences of the emerging mode characteristics. Creative reflection on the life of a church can emerge from such discussion. That can then lead into 'brainstorming' about ways in which movement in the right direction could be brought about. In this way the marks of an emerging church can be used as 'stars to steer by'. A church, sustaining a commitment to move in the direction of the signposts identified in this chapter, will find itself shifting into 'mission mode'.

BEING HUMAN

7

The Prophetic Dimension of the Gospel

Salvation is, essentially considered, the restoration of humanity to mankind.

James Philip, *Christian Maturity.*

God is not about religion, and very much religion, I fear, is not about God. God is about the fulfilment of being human and personal in the glory and celebration of the community of love.

David Jenkins, *Good God!* lecture 4, p.3.

The basic thesis of this book is that one of the striking features of Christianity has been the way that it has adapted both its message and its life style (way of being church) to the changing cultures in which it has taken root, and that this has major implications for the church today. So far we have concentrated on the 'life style' issues, namely how the church has adapted to, and been shaped by the cultures with which it has sought to relate. The implication is that, in a time of major cultural shift through which we are now passing, it will be necessary for the church to develop new ways of being church which relate to modern culture. The basic mark of that new emerging form of church is that it is missionary in nature.

The first step has now been taken to define that shape more clearly by exploring, in the last two chapters, how the church is discovering new ways of being church today. In due course we will return to that theme and explore some practical steps that can be taken by any local church to adjust to the new missionary setting in which the church finds itself.

What has already been said is that spirituality is one of the key components of that emerging way of being church. However, spirituality and gospel are very close relatives. Indeed, since spirituality is born out of a particular understanding of the gospel, we might say that the gospel is the mother, or father, of all spirituality. What you believe and preach is how you see and experience God. For this reason, before proceeding further to consider how change can be brought about in the life of the church, we need to give attention to the gospel; since how we understand the gospel greatly influences the way we build the church.

This discernment of the nature of the gospel is a crucial factor in the work of mission, for the church needs to adapt both its *message* and its *way of being church* to the nature of the culture it is evangelizing. So we need to consider how the gospel is to be expressed in our particular culture, before we can consider how to develop the church which embodies that gospel.

Compromise

At this point in the argument the alarm bells of some readers will be ringing for they will feel that any attempt to 'adapt' the gospel involves compromise, resulting in an inevitable impoverishment of the church and running the risk of heresy. Are not all heresies simply compromises with the prevailing culture and a giving in to the spirit of the age? Such people would further argue that the church has only ever been strong when it has held fast to the 'faith once delivered to the saints'. Only by defending and faithfully proclaiming the unchanging gospel, the eternal truths of God's revelation in Christ, can there be any hope for the church.

That argument sounds convincing, but it fails to do justice either to Scripture or to the experience of the church. The New Testament certainly gives plenty of indications of different attempts to communicate the gospel to different cultures. *Messiah* to the Jews,

Logos to the Greeks, and a good deal of what would pass today as New Age language (Gnostic terminology) in settings such as Colossae (as we will see shortly), all indicate a creativity and originality in the early Church's proclamation of the gospel. *Purpose* to the Romans and *creation* to the Celts only underline that continuing process of listening to particular cultures and learning to speak the gospel in their language and idiom. It was, after all, Martin Luther who said that if our speaking fails to address the precise point at which the world of our times aches, we are not really preaching the Word.

Indeed it is those who have emphasized the 'unchanging gospel' approach who have been least aware of how their understanding is shaped by their own culture, and most guilty of cultural imperialism – all in the name of the gospel.

More than that, the Incarnation itself seems to glory in its 'particularity'. In order to reveal himself to humanity the Eternal and unchanging God chose to express himself in the life of one man, at one time, in one particular setting. Yet he did so in a way that has spoken a universal language of love. God himself clothed his truth in one particular expression.

This creativity in the expression of the gospel has been the mark of the church whenever it has made major inroads into cultures. Certainly, adaptation is a dangerous path which can lead into heresy and compromise, but it does not necessarily lead that way. And those who have resisted change have simply been left like a hulk on the sandbank of time. Fascinating and awesome to see, but of no use if you want to put to sea.

Adaptations

Before considering how we might 'clothe' or incarnate the gospel today, it would be valuable to note some of the ways in which the church has attempted to express its message in new language to new settings, for the fact is that whenever the church has made significant impact on mission, it has clothed the gospel in a way which resonates with the concerns, needs and aspirations of the surrounding community. Indeed doing so is simply expressing the prophetic nature of the gospel by discerning God's specific word to the culture being addressed.

Paul

One striking, and relevant, example from the pages of Scripture is that of the Apostle Paul writing to the Colossians. In the cosmopolitan culture in which he spoke, Paul's use of words is striking. Three in particular stand out, *knowledge*, *fullness* and *mystery*. They were three key words in the prevalent Gnostic religion of his day – a form of religion very similar to much of the New Age movement around today. Rather than avoid such language Paul launches into a daring raid on the vocabulary of the false teachers.

The word gnostic comes from the Greek word meaning to *know*. Gnostics taught that only by secret knowledge (information and initiation) could anyone know the truth. They also taught that the Godhead was a *pleroma* (the Greek for fullness); a veritable menagerie of gods, to whom one could add any you like – such as Christ. At the top of the pyramid was the totally holy, totally Unknowable One. As you descend from the top you get nearer to the earth. At the base are gods who do communicate with earth, but are quite mortal in their unholy instincts and motives. The Gnostics placed Christ somewhere in the middle. Moreover, they said that this *mystery* (hence the term 'mystery religions') was only accessible to those properly in the know (*gnosis*). Such teachers saw the flesh, which includes all the material and physical world, as essentially evil and the spiritual world as essentially holy and good. That is why the Utterly Holy can have no way of communicating with the Utterly Human – except by intermediaries. Any use of these words, *knowledge*, *fullness* and *mystery* in connection with anything to do with physical existence and mere humanity was unthinkable.

Paul, far from abandoning or avoiding all this language, take it on – head on. He takes it over and *fills it with Christian meaning*, as is evident from the following selection of audacious statements by Paul (my italics).

God was pleased to have all his *fullness* dwell in him.

Colossians 1:19.

For in Christ all the *fullness* of the Deity lives in *bodily* form, and you have been given *fullness* in Christ.   Colossians 2:9-10.

To them God has chosen to make *known* among the Gentiles the riches of the glory of this *mystery*, which is Christ in you, the hope of glory.   Colossians 1:27.

In order that they may *know* the *mystery* of God, namely Christ, in whom are hidden all the treasures of *knowledge* and wisdom.

Colossians 2:3.

Here is masterful expression of the good news and truth of Christ, in a mystery religion setting designed to evangelize the hearers through a wholesale resymbolizing of their language.

St Augustine

From the pages of church history, St Augustine of Hippo is a striking example of a Christian seeking to communicate the faith in a new setting. He faced a culture where the political collapse was an expression both of moral decline[1] and also of a deeper discrediting of the contemporary religions. Classical culture had produced two profoundly differing perspectives on the divine. For the Greeks, the gods were all too mortal in their moral choices, even when they cut off each other's heads and turn them into planets. However, they were totally capricious and unpredictable. For the Romans, possibly in reaction to this characteristic of the Greek gods, it was the astrological powers who alone were able to give predictable certainty to life, though at the cost of a passive fatalism – 'whatever will be, will be'. Both these views of the divine had lost credibility by the time of Augustine. There was no overarching religious worldview to hold such a diverse Empire together. In this situation Augustine spoke of the Judeo-Christian God of provi-

[1] See Edward Gibbon, *The Decline and Fall of the Roman Empire*.

dence and history as the one who could give hope and meaning to life. God is working his purposes out. Religion is the submission of our lives to the outworking of that purpose – namely the coming of God's kingdom on earth.

> He [Augustine] bears witness to the faith of Christians that, notwithstanding all appearances, human history does not consist of a series of repetitive patterns, but marks a sure, if unsteady, advance to an ultimate goal. As such it has a beginning, a middle, and an end. In this conviction he finds the marching orders, so to speak, of the *militia* of Christ.[2]

Augustine gave people hope through the call to participate in God's purposes in the world. It 'rang true', and a considerable 'people-movement' resulted, as well as a whole civilization based on Christian principles – Western civilization. Augustine spoke of *purpose*. Purpose and providence were key insights Augustine brought to his culture, and in doing so, laid the foundations of Western civilization as we now have it. It is not without significance that the whole flowering of science has emerged in just such a culture, for the Creator is seen to be a rational and predictable Being whose 'laws' are consistent and can be discovered by careful investigation.

This sense of our being caught up in the purposes of God in history were actually built on a prior understanding of God as person, and of the Trinity.

> Augustine thus discovers in the Trinity a fresh foundation for what we have called the values of the personality ... For, in the Trinity, he discovered a principle capable of saving the reason as well as the will, and thus redeeming human personality as a whole.[3]

It is interesting to note that the terms Person and Personality were originally theological terms developed by Augustine and his contemporaries to describe the nature of God, and hence the nature of mankind made in the image of God. Only in the nineteenth century was the word personality taken over by the emerging science of psychology to describe the nature of human beings. Here again, Augustine laid the foundations on which so much of Western culture is built.

Others

John Wesley clothed the gospel through the language of the 'new birth'. He did so to the working-class culture of his day in particular, finding that this emphasis gave *hope* to people who felt oppressed by their circumstances of life, driven frequently to alcoholism as a way of numbing the hopelessness of life (hence the Methodist emphasis on teetotalism). Such was the extent to which his message resonated with the culture to which he spoke that tens, even hundreds of thousands of people embraced the Christian faith. Moreover, the changed lives resulted in a major reshaping of our culture with the abolition of slavery, the Factory Acts of the nineteenth century, the rise of Trade Unions and the Labour Party and the extension of franchise to every adult, all tracing their origins back to the 'Wesleyan revival'.[4] Some have argued that the Wesleyan revival was what enabled England to avoid the turmoil and suffering of either the French Revolution or the bloody civil war over slavery in America.[5]

In more recent years the striking work of Vincent Donovan[6] in translating the Christian faith into the Masai culture in Africa reflects the same principle of cultural adaptation of the gospel. After one hundred and fifty years of the Catholic Church making no known conversions amongst the Masai tribespeople, Donovan was allowed by his bishop to go beyond, and to go without, the traditional missionary trappings of schools and hospitals and

[4] For a detailed account of the long-term impact of Wesley, see Wesley Murray's *England Before and After Wesley*.
[5] Richard Lovelace, *Dynamics of Spiritual Life*, p.376.
[6] Vincent Donovan, *Christianity Rediscovered*.

simply to sit and listen and express the gospel in terms that related to the Masai people. Within five years over five thousand had become active participants in the faith. What is not so clear, and this has great relevance to the subject of this book, is whether a form of church life was developed that was equally appropriate to that culture.

Prophets

There is a parallel between the models of missionary congregations described in chapter five and the models of missionary messages identified here. The models in Chapter five were of *new ways of being church*. The models in this chapter are of culturally appropriate ways of *expressing the Church's message*. Our need today is to find out how to speak eternal truth in a way that resonates with the needs, hunger and aspirations of our culture. That involves the work of prophets, those who can discern the times and know how to speak into a culture.

This is what is meant by 'enculturating' the gospel. We might equally well speak of incarnating the message. The question is what is that clothed, enculturated gospel for twenty-first century humanity? It is a vital question. Bernard Pawley, a former Archdeacon of Canterbury, addressing General Synod in 1979 when the *Nationwide Initiative in Evangelism* was being launched, said:

The long-suffering clergy do not wish to be told again and again to reinterpret the gospel or make it relevant; they want help in doing it and want to hear what the gospel sounds like and looks like when it has been so treated. There is therefore here a poverty of inspiration which I find a little alarming. It seems to me at this point the whole enterprise betrays its lack of inspiration and needs to be reorientated in one particular classical direction, that of prophecy. If you are going to indulge in evangelism, you have got to have prophets, who to my mind are signally lacking. If you want to do evangelism, first catch your prophet.[7]

The prophetic dynamic of the gospel

Human society has been through various revolutions. The agricultural, industrial, technological and information revolutions have come ever more closely on each other's heels. Yet in the midst of it all we have lost any solid sense of who and why we are. Science has been so conspicuous in explaining the mechanics of everything but has left humanity floundering about the meaning of anything. The Permissive Society and sexual revolution of the sixties encouraged people to 'do their own thing', but when 'anything goes' it seems that nothing goes, nothing works. If you do not know who you are, how can you do *your* thing? For many reasons, not least the vast, impersonal and unresponsive national structures and multi-international corporations, push the individual back on themselves and their own resources.

Furthermore, awareness of our culture's impact on the environment, and of the extent to which it is only sustained by the asset-stripping of many Third World countries, has led to a deep questioning of the whole capitalist economic project. With that questioning goes a search for the lost dimension of the sacred.[8] This search is being carried out in the context of a culture in which people are either out of work or overworked; either discarded or driven by the whole capitalist growth culture. People are left asking the question as to whether 'an upturn in the economy' is a sufficient or satisfactory goal for human existence? It is not so much that the capitalist/democratic culture should be abandoned, but rather that it needs to find an ethical heart and a moral base by which to live. The development of ethical investments and of a strong ethical base in the financial services industry are signs of this hunger. But morality is sustained by both spirituality and

[7] Bernard Pawley, *Report of Proceedings*, July 1979, p.514.
[8] What Peter Berger, in *A Rumour of Angels* calls 'the sacred canopy'.

religious (ultimate) conviction. Our problem is that we do not know where to purchase such commodities.

In this sense of lostness, humanity is in grave danger of being turned in on the self (*incurvatus in se*, as St Augustine defined sin). The very self that was lost, excluded and ignored in Enlightenment and Consumer culture, rediscovers itself in narcissistic consumption:

> The Consumer Society is . . . a flight from human vulnerability, through a channelling of human desire into the amassing of possession.[9]

All of these processes have resulted in a sense of 'moral and spiritual vacuum at the heart of our society' which was somehow brought to the surface in our own country by the manner of the death of James Bulger. It was deeply symbolic, for it was the story of a child lost in the marketplace. Our culture is similarly lost and afflicted by the pursuit of possessions. We are in danger of dying from consumption.

My thesis at this point is that 'what the gospel sounds like and looks like when it has been so treated' is essentially about our *being human*. The Good News, as it relates to our culture, is that being fully human has been demonstrated for us in the person of Jesus Christ, made accessible to us through baptismal incorporation into his death, resurrection, ascension and the gift of the Holy Spirit, and – how wonderful it would be if we could add – is now being incarnately demonstrated at your nearest local church. *The prophetic word for our culture is about God's way of being human.*

Recovering the truth that Christianity is about 'being human' is both good news for Western society and a definition of its agenda that many have come to recognize:

> . . . the great work of our time is for Western man to put his own inner house in order.[10]

[9] John Kavanaugh, *Still Following Christ in a Consumer Society*, p.4.
[?] E.F. Schumacher *Small is Beautiful*

It is not a matter of accepting propositions, but of becoming a new person.[11]

We are invited to join in on God's universal project of sharing and developing love.[12]

Christ creates a new people of God, a new person, a new humanity.[13]

The application of the gospel to contemporary Western culture as it seeks to make sense of a post-Enlightenment, post-modernism view of reality will be found in joining in the search for the humanity we have lost through the very technology that has brought us great riches at the material level and yet such poverty of spirit. If this is so then the mission of the church is to participate in the 'human project'.

Alert to dangers

Before proceeding to give definition and content to an understanding of the gospel in terms of *being human* it is important to identify various ways in which the church can be led astray by such a search. Those most alert to the dangers of compromise are right in that what is being proposed sails very close to 'the spirit of the age'. However, it seems that the Spirit of the Incarnate One is at home in just that place and is able to steer a course around the rocks of compromise and heresy. However, we do well to identify the rocks before setting out on the journey.

First, because we live in a culture where the self is the centre of all that is, and is cut off from others, we have to avoid a spirituality and worldview which are no larger than the human self. 'I am my own divinity' is not just the logic of the self-focused worldview, it

[11] Robin Greenwood, *Transforming Priesthood*, p.132.
[12] David Jenkins, *Good God!* lecture 4, p.3.
[13] Jose Comblin, *Being Human*, p.119.

is the message of much New Age teaching. As such it is a denial of the liberating good news that we are creatures living before the Creator of all that is, who find ourselves through knowing him.

Second, we need to avoid the dangers of being driven further into the corner of a privatized, spiritualized and individualized understanding of truth and the gospel. Many writers alert us to this danger. Richard Lovelace alerts us to this danger in the Christian world when he writes:

> . . . the conclusion that spirituality and social concern are inversely related to one another is unfortunately rather easy to justify from some of the evidence available today. People who are 'into Christianity' may not be into anything else.[14]

The flight into the self has been a significant expression of the marginalizing of religion in recent centuries.[15]

Third, we need an understanding of the human person that takes us beyond the destructive and competitive individualism of the eighties without losing the proper sense of the uniqueness of each person. How we relate to others, and indeed to the whole of human society and to the environment too, needs to find an important place in our understanding and practice of what it means to be human.

Alive to the opportunities

There are dangers in understanding the gospel in terms of the recovery of our lost humanity, but there are great opportunities too. Understanding the gospel in terms of being human can open up to the church two pieces of good news.

It is likely to make for a considerable simplification of the work of the church. If our task is to help each member discover and enter into the fullness of humanity made available to us in Christ, it gives a focus and definition of the life of the church that could well

[14] Richard Lovelace, *The Dynamics of Spiritual Life*, p.356.
[15] From Bryan Appleyard (*Understanding the Present*) quote – note 5 in Chapter two.

lead to considerable simplification in the church's life, and thus to a reduction in the sense of exhaustion that often afflicts clergy and laity alike. That would indeed be good news.

It is likely to be further good news to the church just at the point at which it might feel that to add a mission agenda on top of all the pastoral work we are involved in is likely to be the straw that broke the camel's back rather than a glorious new lease of life. However, an understanding of the gospel as essentially about the restoration of humanity to mankind integrates the internal pastoral life of the church (the discovery, liberation and celebration of the new humanity opened up by Christ) with its external missionary task (to proclaim the truth and availability of the new humanity made possible by Christ). What we are called to *do*, namely to tell and serve others in their search for their true humanity, is also what we are called to *be*, namely those who enjoy and affirm one another in the community of faith as together we make exodus from false values into the wholeness of life made possible through Christ. In this way the whole life of the church becomes at one and the same time both pastoral (building up the faithful) and missionary (proclaiming the faith). Again, to hard-pressed clergy and overstretched laity, this is good news indeed.

8

Exploring the Dynamic of being Human

> Grace is the beginning of glory.
> St Thomas Aquinas.
> Being is being loved.
> G. Marcel.

If 'being human' is the heart of the Christian message to contemporary Western culture, then it requires reflection, prayer and exploration at every level. It would take more than one book, not just one chapter, to explore the subject in depth. It would also, of necessity, be an interdisciplinary exploration involving virtually all the strands of our fragmented physical and social sciences. The goal of this chapter is necessarily much more modest. It is to develop a sufficient framework for what it means to be human to enable us to see how the church should be church in the changing culture in which we live.

What follows is a reading of the creation account of Genesis, in the context of contemporary culture, with a view to discerning some of the broad outlines of what it means to live in the fullness of God's gift of humanity in Christ; knowing ourselves to be made in the image of God. There are four elements in the model which follows. However, as in the whole of life, these overlap and constantly interact. Figure six links these various elements together diagrammatically.

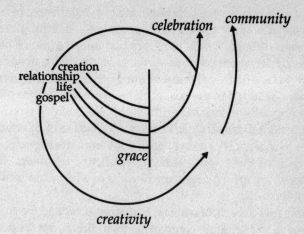

Figure six: the dynamic of living in the image of God.

Grace

To sustain life we need to take in food, air and water. But there are other resources we need; significance, worth, meaning and encounter with love.[1] For humanity is sustained through relationship with the external world of material and social existence. Grace is the word used in the Bible to describe this sustaining source of life. It refers not simply to 'spiritual resources' but rather to how the whole of life is.

The grace-filled nature, or gift, of life covers first the *creational* aspect of life; our own physical existence, material resources and the beauty and wonder which human existence opens up for us. There is also the dimension of *relationships* through which we experience value, worth, a sense of belonging and a developing awareness of our own identity. Our experience of *life* itself, the processes, experiences and phases which we go through and 'what sort of hand' life deals us are also part of what nourishes and

[1] Abraham Maslow, in *Motivation and Personality* was one of the first to analyse this area.

sustains us. As we pass through life we experience, to varying degrees, not only testing and sometimes painful times, but processes through which life gives us hope, a sense of personal worth, achievement and an awareness of 'the divine in our midst'. The *gospel* is a further element in our experience of the grace of all creation. Included in the gospel element are the various means of grace normally associated with church life such as word, sacrament, pastoral care and 'fellowship' through each of which God comes to us and gives us of himself. However, it is important to see that each of these four elements, *creation, relationships, life* and the *gospel*, are means of grace and ways in which God meets with humanity.

These four aspects of *creation, relationships, life* and the *gospel* are, moreover, not separate compartments in life. Scripture points us rather to seeing life in its various depths, not in distinct compartments. So, for example, behind the meteorological factors that determine the cloud pattern, we can be open to see the beauty of the 'skyscape', and in and through that we can glimpse the creativity of the Author of life. At such a moment we touch the presence of God. In that experience the physical, aesthetic and spiritual are layers of reality in the whole experience. That is how we are to see all life, and encounter grace. As Neville Ward has put it:

... every experience is a kind of annunciation.[2]

It is the grace of God in the whole of life to which Genesis points us. Creation is the generous provision of a giving Creator. These gifts touch us most fully when we 'receive them with thanksgiving'.[3] Full humanity, in other words, is experienced when life is consciously received and enjoyed as gift and, thereby as relationship with the Giver. Living eucharistically ('with thanksgiving'[4]) as creatures before the Creator is how life is meant to be lived. It

[2] Neville Ward, *Five for Sorrow, Ten for Joy*, p.3.
[3] 1 Timothy 4:4.
[4] 2 Corinthians 9:11, & 15, Ephesians 5:4 & 20, Philippians 4:6, 1 Thessalonians 5:18, 1 Timothy 4:14.

is, incidentally, a powerful antidote to both a competitive and consumerist mentality.

Those who would touch the depths of the gift of life in this way and learn to live in thanksgiving need help with worship and with prayer through the life of the church.

In worship they need to discover the discipline of stillness from which our culture hides in business, activity and achieving; skating over the surface of life in the rush to get and to get on. Stillness, reflection and meditation are crucial if we are to live in touch with the wholeness of life. Jesus's summary of the two commandments begins with the prior command to '*Hear* O Israel . . .', to enter into the wonder of life as gift, not least through the giving of thanks; for it is in that recognition of the Giver behind the gifts that we touch the heart of the universe. Christian living is, therefore, essentially eucharistic living. This being so, helping people to 'stop, look and listen' is a central role of the church. It was this fact which the highly active Terry Waite discovered in the enforced stillness of his time as a hostage. Not surprisingly he concludes:

> Our fragmented society needs a whole series of 'reflective pools', places where the very deepest issues of life and death may be explored and understood away from the cut and thrust of the market-place.[5]

Help is also needed at the person level, to be people able to receive the grace of God. I have often been asked to give help and advice to churches about the matter of giving. Sometimes I have been told the familiar proverb that 'getting this congregation to give is like trying to get blood out of a stone'. The answer comes back to grace, and to the need to find ways of putting blood into the stone if we are to have any chance of getting some out. In such situations it seems that grace is not getting through.[6] What is true of giving is true in the whole of living. The primary task of

[5] Terry Waite, *Taken on Trust*.
[6] Ezekiel 11:19 makes the fundamental link between spirituality and generosity clear.

the leadership of the church is to help in the receiving of grace, which is why Gerard Hughes is so right when he says:

> Training in prayer should be the main preoccupation and service given by the bishops and clergy to the adult members of the Church.[7]

The importance of the renewable resources of life are being discovered on many fronts today. Economists and environmentalists are pointing out that even more important than a growth economy is a sustainable economy.[8] That is, an economy which does not rob others, the environment or the next generation of the gifts of creation. Crucial to this is finding ways to draw upon the renewable resources in creation (wind, water and sunlight) for the production of electricity. Manufacturing industries equally are learning to draw on the renewable resources of the almost limitless human creativity. Those which do so are developing the highest levels of efficiency and effectiveness.

To be fully alive involves this same openness to the renewable resources of creation, human society and grace that are given to sustain life. Being human, then, begins with *grace* and with the ability to live in *thanksgiving* out of the 'renewable resources' which life opens up to us.

Celebration

Awareness of the goodness of life, humanity, creation and all that is, energizes the human soul for celebration. Celebration is taken here in its widest sense. Worship is part of celebration, but the concept is broader than our normal understanding of worship. It includes the capacity to wonder, to enjoy and take pleasure and delight in God, creation, others, life and, yes, even ourselves. It is the capacity of the child to live in the moment and to enjoy life as a

[7] Gerard Hughes, *God of Surprises*, p.22. See also my book on prayer, *An Affair of the Heart*, which seeks to develop a framework within which such training can be given.
[8] See Meadows & Brundtland, *The Limits to Growth* and *Beyond the Limits*.

gift rather than handle it as some problem to be solved. It may well be why Christ placed a child in the middle of the disciples when he was teaching them about how to *receive* the kingdom. Indeed this capacity to enjoy life as a child is a characteristic of wisdom as described in the Old Testament, and the early Church understood it as a prophecy about Christ.

> Wisdom says: I was beside him like a little child, and I was daily his delight, playing in his presence, continually, rejoicing in the inhabited world and delighting in the human race.[9]

This is where the ending of Genesis Chapter one has seemed to have had such a baleful impact. The chapter break comes at the end of Day Six, rather than Day Seven. Day Six ends with 'man having dominion'. Is that not close to the heart of the ills of Western civilization – its goal is man-in-control? That focus on the supposed climax of creation may well have contributed to the man-centred technological culture which has lost life in its pursuit of control and dominion. The Protestant work ethic has, not surprisingly, arisen out of such a reading of Scripture; indeed, like the doctrine of apartheid it may have been the theological undergirding for the creation of a distorted worldview and culture.

Placing the chapter break where it belongs, after Day Seven, reveals the climax of creation not as man-in-dominion but God-in-celebration. What is now needed is a Protestant play ethic![10] The feasts and festivals (eating and drinking, as well as praising and praying) have an important place in the Jewish roots of the Christian faith. They need to be recovered, and entered into not just for 'church celebrations', but for 'community celebrations'.

A missionary church will be a centre of celebration. Indeed this is already happening. Projects like the nationwide Pentecost celebration, *On Fire*, the importance of the supper element of the

[9] Proverbs 8:30-31.

[10] See Jean Jacques Suurmond's, *Word and Spirit at Play* for a valuable attempt to do just that.

Alpha Course approach to evangelism and nurture, as well as the Great Feast project of the London diocese, point to ways in which the work of evangelism is increasingly being done in the context of celebration. Harvest festivals are an ancient form of celebration that the Church has inherited from its Jewish roots. Those same roots are likely to be the source of many other expressions of celebration. This is why people instinctively look to the church to be the community enabling it to celebrate the gifts of birth and marriage. Even funerals and memorial services have this celebratory element to them in that they are moments to stop to reflect and to give thanks – as well as to grieve. Dennis Potter in his final TV interview before his death from cancer described his understanding of God as 'the feeling of there being something to sing and dance about.'

> Sometimes we hear people say that the highest, noblest form of love is self-sacrifice, that because of the cross, we know that this is what God's love for us is like. The early Church does not teach that the most basic quality of God's love is a suffering self-sacrifice. What first engages God with us is not duty or need or self-sacrifice or obligation or the need to be right or good, but delight in us as beloved.[11]

Celebration is not simply the capacity to sing and dance, to feast and make merry. Authentic celebration, as distinct from hedonistic numbing out, also involves the capacity and willingness to stop and enjoy, rather than rush on to the next thing to get or do. It is the ability to find ourselves by enjoying the goodness of creation, others and life:

> We come to know even ourselves, not through turning inward to study and analyse, but by turning outward to love all that is real and other than ourselves.[12]

Celebration is about 'making all the right connections' with God,

---

[11] Roberta Bondi, *To Pray and to Love*, p.121-2.
[12] Leanne Payne, *The Healing Presence*, p.163.

life, others, all creation – and ourselves. It is about the divine capacity to enjoy God, life and others. Fascinatingly the otherwise almost oppressively serious and earnest Westminster Catechism manages at just one point to break out of its straitjacket of religious correctness at the point where it most matters – its understanding of the purpose of life. To the question, 'What is man's chief end?' the answer given is, 'Man's chief end is to enjoy God and glorify him for ever.'

Brian Keenan, in the midst of sustained dehumanizing effects of captivity, isolation and abuse, grasped the connection between pain and joy, suffering and celebration, humour and humanity:

> There are many things a man can resist – pain, torture, loss of loved one – but laughter ultimately he cannot resist.

> We were convinced by the conditions we were kept in and the lives we managed to lead that if there was a God that God was, above all else, a comedian.[13]

Laughter is one of the deepest forms of the enjoyment of life and celebration of our humanity. It is the celebration of the liberating truth that we are not God, but all too mortal.

Creativity

A response to both grace and celebration is the desire to give expressed in creativity. It could also have been called work, service or ministry. However, 'creativity' is a more holistic and inclusive term. It points to our nature as creatures made in the image of God who both celebrates (Day Seven) and creates (Days One to Six). Such creativity is central to the first creation, and the new creation, understanding of our being made in the image of God. To be human is to share in both aspects of the divine nature, to *celebrate* and to *create*. Creativity is distorted today alike by the consumer culture and by the notion that 'creativity' is what we do in our

[13] Brian Keenan, *An Evil Cradling*, p.269, 172.

'leisure time'. However, to be human is to be creative and we need to practise – and help others to experience – the essential creativity at the heart of all we do and are. Parents create families and family life, clergy create Christian community. Plumbers, teachers, those who work in factories and in offices, politicians and athletes are all engaged in creativity. In the next chapter we will consider destructive forms of 'creativity' which are always ways in which we harness the creative skills and resources to the goal of gaining dominion over others.

Using the term 'creativity' can help to shift the attention of the inherited model of church from an inward looking church-life focus to the outgoing whole-life focus of the emerging church. This shift to a whole-life focus was well expressed recently by the Archbishop of Canterbury:

> A copernican vision is required of us to see at the centre of God's mission not the splendid work of church life but the equally splendid wilderness of the world – where there are few places for Christians to hide, where moral or ethical signposts are blurred or non-existent and where we are outnumbered by the indifference, the unholy and the uncultured despisers of our day. . . It will require a radical change of attitude from us all. It will mean being prepared not to jettison all that we have for the sake of something new and different but of humbly accepting that the local church must come second to the needs of those serving Christ in the world and the real needs of the communities in which we live.[14]

There is a need in the church today for a shift from a focus on 'the work of ministry' to the more important matter of 'the ministry of work'. In Figure six, it is important to note that there is a downward incarnational curve on the creativity line, for it will frequently take us into places of brokenness, pain and suffering in the world; and into confrontation with the structures of power that

[14] Quoted from Yvonne Craig's book, *Learning for Life*, p.1.

bring about that suffering. Creativity, note, also 'lines up with' the grace previously experienced, for the creativity to which we are called involves taking with us the grace we have ourselves encountered. It will often be our only resource – the confidence that grace has sustained us in the past – not the notion that we have all the answers.

Engaging in creativity, both as individuals in the whole of life, and as a church in its corporate activities, is at heart participating in God's mission. The ultimate creativity is the sustaining and renewal of each individual life, all human society, the whole creation and cosmos. Creativity, so understood, is the expression of the dominion (as distinct from domination) that is part of our nature as those made in the image of God. It is the work of the kingdom which Jesus did and called his disciples into. It involves working for justice and peace and for a just sharing of the earth's resources. It will involve confronting the principalities and powers that frustrate the will and goodness of God reaching the life of groups and individuals. It will, of necessity, because it is a spiritual work, require prayer through which we can find God's direction and our part in the midst of a multitude of 'good ideas' and passing enthusiasms.

> Prayer is not a pious instrument by which we move God to baptize our enterprises; it is entering the strength of him who moves history and binds the powers that be.[15]

However, in drawing attention to the spiritual roots of creativity we need to guard against any 'spiritualizing' tendency which would narrow creativity to one sphere of life. All life, all relations, all expressions of artistic ability and human culture are included in the creativity which reflects the image of God in and through us.

A church functioning in the affirmation of its members' creativity will need sufficient pastoral networks for people to be known well enough to discern the areas of creativity to which, in the wider society as well as in the life of the church, they are being

[15] Melba Maggay, *Transforming Society*, p.71.

called. It may well find itself linking with other churches to support groups engaging in particular issues from educational provisions to wealth creation and from the health service to genetic engineering. It is likely to be a church forging partnerships with agencies working in specific areas, such as homelessness, drug abuse or the rehabilitation of offenders. The first sign of its prophetic nature is much more likely to be found in what it is quietly doing than in what it is loudly denouncing; though confrontation is part of the call to bring about creative change. Such a church is, as already noted, likely to travel light as far as its own structures are concerned.

Community

Such creative engagement with the whole of life will inevitably involve working with others. In doing so the church, and the individual Christian, experiences a further dimension of the image of God, namely the social, trinitarian, nature of God. Furthermore, involvement in such creativity as has been previously identified is likely to draw others into an experience of grace and into a desire to celebrate.[16] It is this which is fundamental to the building of community. In this work of community building the church participates in the Trinity, for the dynamic of a missionary congregation living in the image of God expresses the nature of the God revealed in the person of Christ – *giving, celebrating, creative* and *love-in-community*. Tragically this is what in international, national, industrial and domestic affairs, our world so often lacks; namely the gift of life-giving community.

> Unable to engage our interior lives, we are incapable of engaging the interior lives of other people. Not knowing ourselves, we are unable to reveal who we are before the face of another person. And we are unable to receive them in their personhood since we are out of touch with our own.[17]

[16] This is a very similar pattern to the 'service, worship, discipleship' of the *Isaiah vision*, though the order here is different.

[17] John Kavanaugh, *Still Following Christ in a Consumer Society*, p.8.

> Trapped in our tradition of rugged individualism, we are an extraordinarily lonely people. So lonely, in fact, that many cannot even acknowledge their loneliness to themselves, much less to others.[18]

To this end, the development of communities of faith is crucial. Too easily, as was said in identifying the chief marks of the church in inherited mode, we see the church as an organization rather than a community.

> At the same time, the political, social, and economic institutions of government are changing radically as well. Larger and more impersonal, they are increasingly competitive, specialized, bureaucratic, and out of touch with the people. Created to serve humanizing forces within society, they tend to evolve into alienating structures with dehumanizing programs.[19]

As networks rather than institutions are the means through which people increasingly relate to one another, it is vital that the church itself discovers how to become a network of loving relationships. In this process it will need to discover how to be an empowering, forgiving and conflict-handling community. For many who have lacked stable relationships, the church may well find itself fulfilling the role of family and natural community in a setting when both of them have collapsed. It will not be easy and will require a significant amount of its skilled leadership to be active in this area whilst simplifying all the time its organizational structure.

Reflections

Several concluding comments need to be made:

First, there is an *essential flow* and movement in this dynamic of being human. The flow of *grace, celebration, creativity* and *com-*

[18] Scott Peck, *The Difference Drum*, p.58.
[19] John Westerhoff III, *Living the Faith Community*, p.8.

munity are like four themes of a piece of music or four colours in a piece of material. They weave in and out of each other, and it is both their existence in the design and the interplay of their relationships which create the particular work of art. These are the four themes of our humanity and of a church seeking to live in this dynamic. They need to be the focus of leadership in the emerging church. That church will need leaders developing the skill of creating communities which harmonize this music of our humanity for the blessing and the survival of the surrounding community. They will need to learn to play such music in a way that touches the hearts of those who hunger to have cause for celebration, creativity and community.

Second, *several major themes of Scripture* can be seen as expressed in the diagram presented in this chapter. From the Old Testament three great themes connect with what has been said here at the following points. *Sabbath* expressed the *celebration* of God on Day Seven. It is also a recurrent theme expressing rest, enjoyment and liberation from work. *Jubilee* picks up that theme but expresses also the great *creativity* of God's grace and goodness. Certainly it was a fundamental theme behind the whole of Jesus's understanding of his ministry.[20] His work was one of setting captives free. *Shalom* (Hebrew for peace) is a further Old Testament theme which corresponds with the *community* aspect of being human, for it expresses the blessing which comes when everything, and everyone, is in their right place. It is about harmony, balance and order.

The flow of this understanding of what it is to be human can also be understood, from a New Testament perspective in particular, as an expression of the two great commandments to love God (celebrating Him, sharing in His creativity and His nature as community), and to love others (by joining with them in celebration, being creative with and for them and being brought to true community in love with them).

Third, *the life of Jesus* makes it abundantly clear that such a way

[20] Luke 4:18-19, Isaiah 61:1-2, Leviticus 25:8-55.

of being human happens not as a result of superhuman effort but rather by faith-filled dependence on God as gracious Father. Jesus's living out of the fullness of his humanity was sustained by the constant weaving of a listening obedience to the Father, into the fabric of daily life. This availability to God, and active putting of himself into the purposes of God, is expressed in such Scriptures as:

> Man does not live on bread alone, but on every word that comes from the mouth of God.
>
> Matthew 4:4

> My mother and brothers are those who hear God's word and put it into practice.
>
> Luke 5:2

> 'My food,' Jesus said, 'is to do the will of him who sent me and to finish his work.'
>
> John 4:34

> Jesus gave them this answer: 'I tell you the truth, the Son can do nothing by himself; he can do only what he sees his Father doing'.[21]
>
> John 5:19

This engaging with God and his purposes is expressed diagramatically (see Figure seven) in two ways. The overarching line of the *Trinity* points to the fact that being human is to live in openness to God. The undergirding line of *listening/obedience* reflects the availability to God demonstrated in the life of Christ. This open availability to the purposes of God (the *missio dei*) is expressed in the Lord's Prayer by praying for the coming of his kingdom and doing of his will, before addressing our needs.[21] The curve of this listening/obedience line reflects the call of God upon the life of the believer to plumb the depths of love in obedience to the Father – the downward mobility of incarnation leading to the upward mobility of resurrection life as graphically portrayed in Philippians 2:6-11.

To be human is to live as creatures before the Creator – not to live shut up to our own wisdom and limitations. The task of the

---

[21] See my *An Affair of the Heart*, Chapter 10.

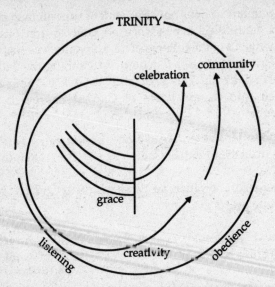

Figure seven: listening obedience as the way to full humanity seen in Christ.

Church is to be the community where this humanity is being lived out and made accessible to all. This is what a church renewed in mission will be about.[22]

---

[22] It is helpful to put the framework for being human, which I have developed in this chapter, into a three-dimensional model in which each of the layers identified by John Reader are operative. In *Local Theology*, pp.18-22, he develops a four-layered framework for the *structure of a contemporary spirituality* of the unconscious, the practical-consciousness, the critical-consciousness and the transrational-consciousness.

9

Sin – The Gravity of Our Situation

> To have a weak understanding of sin is part of our being sinners.
>
> *S. Kierkegard.*

> Sin is man's determination to manage by himself.
>
> *Rudolf Bultmann.*

The goodness of creation is a vital starting point in our exploration of all that is. Hence the focus of the last chapter on all that is good about being made in the image of God. Yet all that has been said so far about being human has left out one major dimension of the human condition, namely the presence of evil and its impact on the whole created order. This temporary omission has been an intentional choice, for if there has been a breakage, we need to know the original design before restoration can take shape. Moreover, there has been a strong negative, world-rejecting streak within Christianity which needs to be avoided. Any sense of a dualism, between the goodness of 'spiritual things' and the sinfulness of 'human things', must be avoided.[1]

However, to deny the reality of evil is no solution. The dark side

---

[1] Matthew Fox in *Original Blessing* and *Creation Spirituality*, argues for just this affirmative starting point, but weakens his case against the dualism in much Christian thinking by setting up a dualism of his own between creation-spirituality and a redemption-fall perspective. This chapter is essentially an attempt to show how the two fit together rather than fight each other.

of human existence is all too evident to us today, not least through the impact of the media. It touches the whole of life, from inner personal self-understanding and unconscious drives, through the pain of human relationship at the levels of marriage, industrial relationships and political structures, and into structures of injustice and what Paul calls 'principalities and powers'. The twentieth century began with such optimism about 'progress', yet for all our scientific advances and spread of education and democracy, we have witnessed some of the worst atrocities of history. The Gulags of the Soviet Union, the concentration camps of the Nazis, the devastation of Hiroshima and the bitter 'tribal wars' of Bosnia and Rwanda in recent years, point to deep roots of fear, hatred and destructiveness in the human heart.

The dangers of not believing in gravity

This destructive force in human experience can be likened to gravity in nature. It is both the force that 'pulls us down' and the presence which makes us, like the plants, 'grow up'. However, it is not only pride that comes before a fall, so does not believing in gravity. That is where much of our culture is at present. Pop psychology has shifted so far into self-actualization and self-fulfilment that it has lost all capacity to own human frailty, accept responsibility and move. Of over six hundred books with the word 'Self-' in the title, only two were found to have anything to say on the subject of self-criticism or consideration of the possibility that, sometimes, I am wrong.

Modern consumer culture has bought into the disbelief in gravity by projection of responsibility at every stage onto someone else. In a recent case in America someone successfully sued McDonald's for over a million pounds because their coffee was too hot and scalded them as they were opening the container while holding it between their knees in a moving car!

New Age spirituality often reflects this same unwillingness to deal with distorted views of self, life, God and others, which come from the unhealed psyche. Jungian psychology, drawing as it does on Gnostic insights, also attempts to marry good and evil.

It is one of the strengths of the Christian faith that it has a framework within which to face, own and deal with this dark side to life. It is of particular importance in a culture that tends to abdicate responsibility, blaming the government. However, all too easily the Church has lost its nerve and its way at just this point.

> During the late nineteenth century, while the church's understanding of the unconscious motivation behind surface actions was vanishing, Sigmund Freud rediscovered this factor and recast it in an elaborate and profound secular mythology. One of the consequences of this remarkable shift is that in the twentieth century pastors have often been reduced to the status of legalistic moralists, while the deeper aspects of the cure of souls are generally relegated to psychotherapy.[2]

It is in a recovery of its understanding of, and ability to deal with this darkness of human existence that the Christian faith may well have most to contribute to today's culture. If we are to be 'physicians of a civilization of love' we will need to avoid 'healing the wounds of my people lightly'.[3] In Christ we have a model of one whose expression of love involved the courageous confrontation of pride, prejudice and dishonesty especially in high places as well as in breaking in with the good news of the kingdom to the disadvantaged and marginalized victims of structures of evil. He always did this by setting free and empowering, never by attempting to control others through the imposition of a religious power which, like so many 'revolutions' in history changed the role of oppressors and victims but not the vicious cycle of that oppression.

The nature of sin

The biblical language has a rich vocabulary with which to grasp the gravity of the human predicament. Sadly, today the word 'sin'

[2] Richard Lovelace, *Dynamics of Spiritual Life*, p.88.
[3] Jeremiah 6:14.

has a shallow and distorted meaning in popular culture largely related to sexual wrongdoing. Biblical understanding points beyond outward behaviour to the distorted motivations of those actions.

> In its biblical definition, sin cannot be limited to isolated instances or patterns of wrongdoing: it is something much more akin to the psychological term *complex;* an organic network of compulsive attitudes, beliefs and behaviour deeply rooted in our alienation from God.[4]

The twin roots of that complex are presented as pride and unbelief. The pride which is determined to play God in every situation and the unbelief that is convinced God will not do so. Pride and unbelief reject the idea of humanity as a call to live as a creature before the Creator. Indeed they reveal that the heart of this complex is a denial of the reality of God as the centre of existence and all that is, and the rejection of what it means to be human. Sin is acting out of character as those made in God's image, it is all that is contrary to his nature as it is expressed in each unique situation.

However, there is a deeper diagnosis running through Scripture, particularly in the ministry of Jesus and the message of Paul. This is the view of sin as a power. This is the background to the exorcisms which Jesus performed, releasing people from a power that controlled them. Equally, Paul, particularly in Romans, sees evil as a force that takes control of human existence and from which liberation is required (see especially Romans Chapters 1 and 7). Whilst this power is uncovered at the personal level in the ministry of Jesus, it is unmasked at the cultural and structural level by Paul in what he says about the principalities and powers. Evil is a power that has a habit of 'getting us', and like gravity, of 'getting us down'.

Becoming human

Only within the framework of an understanding of the reality of

---

[4] Richard Lovelace, *Dynamics of Spiritual Life*, p.88.

evil can it be seen that we are involved in a battle to become human. None of us has arrived. The Christian community exists, not as a rest home for 'new arrivals', but as staging posts along the road of becoming, for:

> Few Christians are ever fully evangelized. All our lives we need the power of the gospel to transform us.[5]

How that battle makes itself evident, and where the gravity of our situation shows, can be illustrated within the framework of the previous chapter in which we developed a model of being human. How sin pervades the whole human project, and how that reality is to affect the missionary nature of the church, can now be explored.

If being human is made possible through the sustaining resources of grace, then a double distortion can be detected at this point. One aspect of that distortion is the loss of sustaining resources which can often result in a person being traumatized by their experience of what is intended to sustain.

A famine victim experiences *creation* as enemy and robber, not as gift. The abused child experiences *relationships* as afflicting and destructive, rather than as affirming and creative.[6] Moreover, it is not just in cases of clear physical or sexual abuse that the child is robbed of the gift of life. The child in any codependent family setting, or where identity is focused around achieving rather than personal value, experiences many good gifts mixed up with dangerous distortions. Wounds at the family level are deep afflictions.

Equally, people's experience of *life* and the major processes and stages that go to make it up can be deeply destructive. 'Anna did not have a childhood, she had a nightmare . . .' as one story of growing up began.

Tragically, even the *gospel* resource can partake of the nature of gravity and drop upon a person as the dead hand of controlling, authoritarian legalism. When done in the name of God and the

---

[5] *Rite of Christian Initiation of Adults*, (St Thomas More Centre) p.14.
[6] Alice Miller, *The Drama of Being a Child*, and *For Your Own Good*.

gospel it leaves not only deep wounds, but serious distortions that frequently leave a person controlled by shame. Shame is different from guilt. Guilt says 'I did wrong,' shame says 'I am wrong.' Guilt says 'I have failed,' shame says 'I am a failure.'

So, in the experience either of the deprivation or the distorting intrusion of the gifts of grace designed to sustain life, evil can manifest itself as a deep wound. However, there is another form of distortion prompted not from without, but from within. Within all of us there is an instinct that prompts us to a wilful choosing of what is wrong – destructive of us and of others. In this case, it is we who freely turn gifts of grace to our own, and others, harm. In taking (grasping) rather than receiving (with thanksgiving) we become abusers of life's gifts: '[they] . . . worshipped and served the created things rather than the Creator' (Romans 1:29). How this works out in practice can be seen at each of the aspects of what it means to be human which were identified in the previous chapter (see Figure eight p. 134)

Idolatry: distorted grace

When we grasp the gifts of life for ourselves rather than see them as the gifts of a generous Giver, we turn them into ends rather than means to a higher end. When that happens the creature, rather than the Creator, becomes the focus of our life's orientation. We give thanks *to* the gifts rather than *for* them. This failure to see beyond the gifts to the Giver, results in our worship of created things.[7] This is the heart and essence of idolatry.

Thanksgiving expresses the truth that neither we nor other creatures are the centre of the universe. In fact, in thanksgiving we go beyond ourselves to affirm, give honour to and take delight in all that is not ourselves.

> Praise expresses the marvel of not being the centre of the universe ourselves.[8]

[7] Romans 1:25, Ephesians 5:5, and 2 Timothy 4:4.
[8] Cardinal Carlo-Maria Martini, *What Am I That You Care For Me?* p.73.

Thanksgiving is also an expression of the human instinct to 'centre' our lives. By doing so we embrace a focus outside of ourselves by which to give meaning and purpose to life.

> . . . the human creature is one that inevitably centres itself in this world and does so by choice . . . Idolatry, in simple terms, is the choice of treating as ultimate and absolute that which is neither absolute nor ultimate.[9]

However, when we put our focus on secondary things, however good within themselves, then we make them a god. That is so not only in the more obvious cases of people driven by a lust for power or for possessions. It is also true when anything other than God gains the central focus of living. Even the ideas we have about God can turn into idols. Certainly ideas themselves, in the world of academics, can become objects of worship.

It is at just this point that the power of evil becomes evident, for idols have a way of taking us over. What we freely choose to give ourselves to has the power to control us.

> . . . my god is that which rivets my attention, centres my activity, preoccupies my mind, and motivates my action.[10]

Such power is never abused when our life focus is on the enjoyment of God. It is, ultimately, always abused when anything else becomes our focus. There is here a double destructiveness. Anything, however good, does us harm if it becomes our idol. It also is drained of its goodness, and becomes a thief and a robber to the one who worships it.[11]

Addiction: distorted celebration

The gravity of sin in human existence distorts the call to celebrate, turning the capacity to *enjoy* all things into a need to *possess* them.

[9] Luke Johnson, *Sharing Possessions*, p.49-50. See particularly pp.43-55 for a fine treatment of the whole subject of idolatry.
[10] Luke Johnson, *Sharing Possessions*, p.49.
[11] John 10:8.

Thanksgiving is acknowledgement of the One from whom all good gifts come. Celebration is the enjoyment of those gifts before the One who gives, and in line with the character of the One who gives. However, when we enjoy the gifts of God as ends in themselves they turn to *addictions*.

In popular thought alcohol, drugs and, more recently, work are seen as addictive. However, the range is considerably wider. There are three major types of addiction.

Substance addictions include not only drugs and alcohol, but tobacco, caffeine and chocolate, and anything that can control us in this way. Not that these are necessarily always addictive. *Process* addictions cover such areas as work, shopping and sexual experience. Sex addicts, for example, are in love with the process, the experience, rather than the person. *Relationship* addictions cover the whole area of codependency and the issues of power and control over others on which some people feed their souls.[12]

The life of the Church is particularly prone to the effects of process and relationship addictions. It is in the church as healing community we need to find the acceptance of ourselves for ourselves alone, the loving strength to confront these distorting forces and a place where we can face reality for, as T.S. Eliot said, 'Mankind can bear very little reality.' Too often the church is the last place where either unjudging love or real truth are faced. When they are, the church becomes a centre of healing for all around it. This is where, when the agenda of the church becomes the sustaining of one another in the fulfilment of our humanity, that three 'tasks' flow together. First, the true pastoral work of helping each other to wholeness and holiness. Second, the church becoming a place where the gospel is lived. Third, the equipping of the church for its role in the whole of society to establish a 'civilization of love' in which the principles and experiences of the first two tasks are taken out in the whole of society as the church's contribution to the 'welfare of the city'.[13]

[12] See work of Pia Melody, *Facing Co-dependency* and *Breaking Free*.
[13] Jeremiah 29:7

Domination: distorted creativity

In terms of the gift of creativity, the distorting effect of evil shows up as the drive to dominate and control others and the whole creation. Our Western culture is a classic example of the way that creativity slips so easily into domination. Creativity brings life; it is a way of channelling the grace of God to the whole created order. Domination takes life, takes control and is a way of robbing others of life and the resources necessary for living. The impact of the rich North on the Third World and the environment is eloquent testimony to the destructive nature of such 'control'.

The gift of being made in the image of God is the authority to have 'dominion'. It is seemingly so close to 'domination' but actually so far. It is the difference between Jesus who spoke with authority and the way that the authorities spoke by destroying him. One gives life, the other kills. It is abuse of power which is so central to the human predicament. It has a spiritual dimension. An important part of Christian discipleship has to do with the confronting of distortion of human creativity.[14] It is at just this point that Christians engage

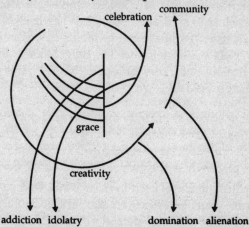

Figure eight: the effect of gravity on the gift of being human.

[14] See Lesslie Newbigin, *The Gospel in a Pluralistic Society*, Chapter 16, and Walter Wink's trilogy on The Principalities and Powers.

with God's mission in the world. A vital focus of the emerging church is on helping church members to discern this distorted creativity and to know how to overcome such evil.

Alienation: distorted community

When it comes to our being made, in the likeness of God, to be social beings, the destructive nature of evil manifests itself as the gravity which causes us to be pulled into the negative. This can best be described as alienation, though it has a multitude of faces.

Alienation, in its most obvious form, cuts us off from others. We live apart from others. However, this is, in the final issue, an unnatural position and almost invariably is not sustainable. Our relationship with others is rather like a person on the end of a strong elastic rope. The further we run from relationships the quicker we reach the point at which the rope is at full stretch. At that point inner forces take over and impel us back – destructively. This has recently been graphically, and destructively, manifested in people (usually men) who have shot or knifed people at random – usually in groups such as in shops and schools. When friends and neighbours are interviewed after such incidents they usually say, 'He seemed perfectly normal, but he kept himself to himself.' Tragically he could not 'keep himself to himself'; it is contrary to human nature made in the image of the Trinity.

> Humanization is a reciprocal thing. We cannot know ourselves or declare ourselves human unless we share in the humanity of another . . . We needed the stimulus of another person, his sympathy, his critical judgement to help guide us.[15]

Alienation also manifests itself in other ways. Dull conformity to group norms often expresses an outward sociability which is disconnected from the real person within. Churches too often welcome such people and use them as the willing workhorses of their endeavours,[16] rather than seeking to bring healing between

[15] Brian Keenan, *An Evil Cradling*, p.287.

the outward social being and the true inner being of the person.

A further expression of alienation is to be seen in the person who appears to be fully 'socialized' yet handles all relationships in a distorting or manipulative way. Inner pain, instead of being addressed is rather projected, and surrounding social relationships muddied as a result.

The cross in the crisis

The church that is ordering its life around participation in God's mission in the world, will find itself continually drawn into the places of brokenness, pain and conflict. These are the points at which the gravity of our human predicament is manifesting itself. Often this is happening in a crisis situation – a place of conflict and change where things could go either way.

> . . . when testing comes and choices are made in that part of us where good and evil rage in mortal combat, the people of this kingdom reach within themselves for their highest and deepest allegiances and make their stand.[17]

The Chinese symbol for crisis is the conflation of two other symbols, those for *danger* and *opportunity*. To seek first the kingdom of God is to see the opportunity in the danger, and to embrace the danger with the opportunity. Jesus did that as much in his touching of the people with leprosy as he did in setting his face steadfastly to go up to Jerusalem.

God's mission can be described as the work of turning addiction into thanksgiving, idolatry into celebration, domination into creativity and alienation into community. We see this happening where Christians care for the homeless and bereaved, where they confront injustice and exploitation, where they defend the environment against the destructive forces of the consumer culture, where they work for reconciliation between groups and cultures, where they befriend and defend the marginalized.

[17] Melba Maggay, *Transforming Society*, p.36.

This is the work of the kingdom for which we pray in the Lord's Prayer. It is the way in which Jesus has shown us to a profound degree what it means to live creatively, and to win in the battle against evil:

> Do not be overcome by evil, but overcome evil with good.[18]

This 'overcoming' is the radical nature of the Christian social and moral agenda. Paul, in the above quotation puts the alternatives so starkly. We either overcome or are overcome. There is no neutrality. Yet so much social protest and revolution involve only the change in who is the oppressor and who the oppressed.

It is at this point that gravity can be seen as a gift. It is so often in the pain and struggle and brokenness of life that grace, mercy, truth and humanity break through. The plant is most truly itself because it has to stand strong against the gravity. As Brian Keenan observed:

> Perhaps all art is created out of malformity.

> Captivity had re-created freedom for us.[19]

And in similar vein:

> That is why I turn back to the years of my imprisonment and say . . . 'Bless you prison' . . . I nourished my soul there. 'Bless you, prison, for having been in my life!'[20]

The church is the place where such a calling is renewed, reflected upon and where it finds new energy for such a task. That energy comes out of the energizing presence of God in worship.

The healing of the nations

This overcoming of evil with good, by turning back the tide of

---

[18] Romans 12:21. See also Romans 8:28-39, the repeated theme of *overcomers* in Revelation (2:7,11,17,26,3:5,12,21,21:7).

[19] Brian Keenan, *An Evil Cradling*, pp.xvi and 230.

[20] A. I. Solzhenitsyn, *The Gulag Archipelago II*.

addiction, idolatry, domination and alienation into the life-giving flow of thanksgiving, celebration, creativity and community is at the heart of the redeeming work of Christ and the mission of the Church. Gravity is overcome by resurrection. His life has shown us how love overcomes evil. His death and resurrection have opened up to humanity a way of defeating those very forces that would seem determined to destroy us. It is this work of overcoming evil which is central to the *missio dei*, God's mission in human society.

As much in his befriending of the lepers and marginalized as in his teaching about the kingdom to his disciples and in his confrontation with the principalities and powers of Church and State in his passion, Jesus's creativity was expressed in this cosmic warfare.

So too the Christians, in their personal lives, in the life of the faith community and in their engagement with the whole social setting in which we are placed, are called to the same work. Indeed, rightly understood this is what the Church's worship is all about. As John Robinson puts it:

> Liturgy is at its heart social action. The very term 'liturgy' derives from two Greek words, *laos* and *ergon*, meaning 'people' and 'work'. Liturgy is public work – and, indeed, in its original secular context 'public works' . . . This is the point where all Christian action begins, where we are united with his act, and where what he has done *for* us is renewed *within* us for transmission to the world. This is the crucible of the new creation, in which God's new world is continually being fashioned out of the old, as ordinary men and women are renewed and sent out as the carriers of Christ's risen life.[21]

Judgment

A fascinating commentary on, and confirmation of, the dynamic of being human and the distorting effect of evil spelt out in these last two chapters are provided by the teaching of Jesus on the judgment at the end of time. The way of seeing what it means to be

[21] John Robinson, *Liturgy Come To Life*, pp.14-16.

made in the image of God as portrayed in Genesis at the beginning of human history reappears as the *basis of judgment* at the end of time. In Matthew's gospel[22] the words of Jesus are recorded about the judgment of both Jerusalem, and of all humanity. A call to be a wise and faithful servant is made as the End approaches. Then come three parables about the basis of that judgment.

The first parable, of the ten virgins, is about being ready to *celebrate*. The foolish virgins have been seduced by the busyness of life and have come to celebration in an unprepared way. They have been living to work, not working to live. Judgment falls on them because of their lack of readiness, their failure to take seriously the call to play, to enjoy, and to celebrate the Bridegroom – the point of it all.

The second parable, of the talents, is about being willing to work – *creatively*. It is not the amount of creativity which has been achieved that is the basis of judgment, but rather the unwillingness to take risks in the pursuit of appropriate industry. They have buried not just their treasure, but a part of themselves, their ability to 'make something of their lives'. Judgment falls on those who suppress their creative gifts and calling.

The third parable, of the sheep and goats is about willingness to make *community*. The ones who reflect the likeness of the Father in heaven are those who feed the hungry, visit the prisoners and clothe the naked. They create a community of faith and love by their actions. Judgment falls on those who look after themselves and will not put themselves out to bring others into the household of faith. Judgment falls on those who will not create community.

In this way we see from the beginning (Genesis 1) to the End (Matthew 23-25). Moreover, in this section of Matthew's Gospel we are shown the beginning – the purpose of life – from the perspective of the judgment of the End. To celebrate the One, to be creative and make community are what it means to be human. It is also the basis of judgment in the End, for as St Irenaeus put it many centuries ago:

> The glory of God is a human being fully alive,
> and the end of being human is the glory of God.

22 Matthew 23-25.

BEING CHURCH

10

Forward in Faith

At all times the Church carries the responsibility of
reading the signs of the time and of interpreting them
in the light of the gospel.

Vatican II.

The need of the local faith community is to begin to
develop an appropriate form of contemporary spirituality.

John Reader, *Local Theology* p.9.

Now is the time to address practical issues. Just how can this shift
from the inherited to the emerging model of church life take place?
Where do we begin? What do we do? And how can we distinguish
which are the important issues needing to be addressed? How, in
other words, is the church to move *forward in faith*, living it out and
sharing that faith with the world around it?

The next chapter will deal with another set of questions about
where to begin in making such a shift. Should we try to change the
whole life of the local church or should we start afresh or with a
willing group? Indeed, do we need to abandon existing structures
or should we proceed by way of seeking to renew them? However,
this chapter focuses rather on the major areas of change needed for
the missionary nature of the church to emerge.

Framework for change

The framework within which the various aspects will be considered is the one used in Chapter three to express the spiritual heart of the life of a faith community. This time there are two important additions to the diagram (see Figure nine below). First, the whole is put in its proper context of the world and culture in which the church is set. Second, the lines between the various aspects have been made permeable to express the fact that each aspect is to influence and shape every other aspect. We are not dealing with either a disembodied church, unconnected to its particular setting, nor with separate compartments which can be seen as complete within themselves.

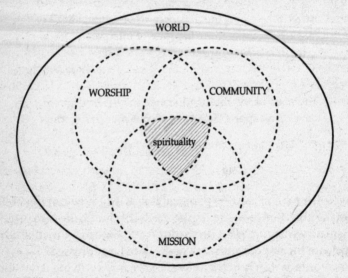

Figure nine: framework for facilitating change.

There is a clear logic in beginning to consider the changes by paying attention first to the world (the setting of the church) and then to the spirituality (the message of the church) which appropriately expresses the faith in that particular setting. Thereafter, what to pay attention to will depend almost entirely on local situation. One area may be most pressing and in dire need of attention. Equally, the opposite may be true. There may be an aspect of the church's life which the church feels secure about and with which it can therefore most readily deal.

The various models of emerging churches outlined in Chapter five illustrate this point. The starting point for the *Isaiah vision* is with a mission agenda, whilst in *Liturgy Come To Life* it was in worship. For *Base Communities* it was the world-context issue which caused the community aspect to emerge first, as in the case of *Open Doors Open Minds*, whilst with *The Blessing*, spirituality was the starting point. For *Local Theology* it was the world-context issue which led primarily to a reworking of the understanding and practice of mission. What matters is not so much where a church starts as that, by the end of the process, the whole life of the church has been renewed in mission.

Given the flexibility and openness to different local application identified above, it does, nonetheless, seem valuable to suggest a three-stage model (suitably and flexibly applied in the local situation – see next chapter) for the renewal of the church in mission.

Stage one: developing an earthed spirituality

If, as has already been argued, spirituality is at the heart of church life, then that is a natural starting point. The whole thrust of this book is that that cannot happen in isolation as a sealed compartment of life, but rather must arise out of the church seeking to engage with the culture around it. Hence the use of the term 'earthed'. The gospel has to be incarnated in a particular context.

> . . . evangelism needs a context, a setting in which the things we say about Jesus become truly incarnate . . . It is precisely because the church has retreated from the world that the gospel now lacks a context.[1]

and

> A spirituality that bypasses awareness of and involvement in

[1] Melba Maggay, *Transforming Society*, p.20-21.

social and political issues is not really engaging the full human being and is, thus, incomplete.[2]

The three chapters in the section **Being Human** is one attempt to do just this. It has been developed out of listening to the questions around in our culture. It seeks to develop a dialogue between gospel and culture. In that dialogue, culture will present a critique of the church, its way of operating and its understanding of the truth. This dialogue is a two way process in which the church will then seek to present a critique of the surrounding culture with gospel values. That critique will be expressed primarily by the living of gospel values.

This process of developing an earthed spirituality is marked by listening and by articulation.

The *listening* needs to happen at a global and a local level. It is important to have both these angles on the subject as today's culture is both a patchwork of different sub-groups and also a global village. In listening to the 'local community' it is important to identify the local culture from a social grouping perspective, not just from a geographical one. At the same time it is important to be aware of the major national and global trends, since, for example, consumer culture affects our whole national life wherever we live. Certainly an increasing number of cultures in the world are being shaped by the market economy and by consumerism.[3]

Members of the church with reflective skills need to be drawn into leadership to make their contribution. A missionary congregation will give high value to those who are engaged on the church-world frontiers and who will know the real issues within the local area.

A major, though neglected, aspect of listening is lamentation. It involves a reflective listening to the pain and brokenness of the world and the bringing of that before God in intercession. It is a form of prophetic insight that leads on to hope rooted in the coming of God's kingdom.[4] Two of the most eloquent and emotive passages in Scripture come out of this dynamic:

[2] John Reader, *Local Theology*, p.22.
[3] See J.K. Galbraith, *The Culture of Contentment*.
[4] See Walter Breuggemann, *The Prophetic Imagination*.

I have seen the affliction of my people who are in Egypt, and have heard their cry because of their taskmasters; I know their sufferings, and am come down to deliver them.

O Jerusalem, Jerusalem, killing the prophets and stoning those who are sent to you! How often would I have gathered your children together as a hen gathers her brood under her wings, and you would not![5]

Such listening prayer is fundamental to mission. It is as we see things from God's perspective that we discover his agenda and priorities and discover hope, which is at the heart of all spirituality. Moreover, it points us to the fact that true listening has a prayer dimension to it. It is often in prayer about problems, such as the homeless or the increase of crime, that vision is discovered about what action the church is being called by God to take.

The *articulation* that needs to take place is of an appropriate spirituality in response to the context. There are several issues here. The first is to identify whether the situation calls for the creation of an appropriate spirituality or the articulation of one that is already present. Some situations, for instance, in some completely new church plant ventures or, in churches where collapse of membership has taken place or where a spiritual heart has been lost, we are likely to need to develop, or create, a 'new spirituality'. However, much more frequent is the task of articulating what is already present.

This *articulation* has value for several reasons. It gives shape and form to often unconscious assumptions and attitudes rather along the lines of the person who said, 'How can I know what I think until I hear what I say?' Bringing the core values of the church (another way of seeing and identifying 'spirituality') into the light means that they can then be assessed as to how adequate they are. Articulating the spirituality of a church is a very effective form of equipping for mission. The medieval mystics taught that evangelism is 'sharing the fruits of our contemplations with others'. The

[5] Exodus 3:7-8, and Matthew 23:37 (both RSV).

church's struggle with evangelism today may well be due to a lack of contemplation. Certainly, articulation of a church's spirituality involves contemplation. It is, however, digging for deeply refreshing, though often hidden, fruit.

In seeking to work with churches, I have developed the definition (quoted above, p.86), of the often slippery matter of spirituality.

> . . . spirituality is our understanding and experience of how we encounter God, and how that encounter is sustained.

I have found the following framework useful in trying to get hold of a church's spirituality.

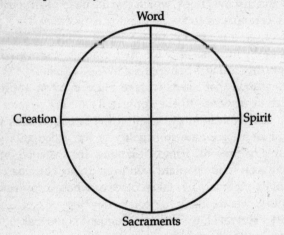

Figure ten: spirituality framework.

The four points of this compass relate to the four major traditions within the Church. The *Word* is how the Protestant/evangelical tradition focuses its faith. The *Spirit* is the focus of the Pentecostal/charismatic tradition. The *Sacraments* are the key to the Catholic/Orthodox understanding of the faith. The fourth tradition, called here *Creation*, expresses the focus of the faith of the Liberal tradition. It includes those whose starting point is social action, the use of reason, or those whose primary focus is on what is now called 'creation spirituality'. Churches that draw directly on just one of those traditions will find one of the four arms of this diagram expressing the heart of their spiritual life. However, many churches include a mixture. So, for example, the fan-shaped, shaded area (in Figure eleven) starts between two of the compass points, and reflects, in this case, an evangelical/charismatic spirituality. Obviously a spirituality can start from any point on the compass.

I have come increasingly to the view that what each church needs to do is to develop an *enriched core* to its spiritual life. Maybe it is appropriate to do so in the nuclear age in which we live. Both words in that phrase are important. The *core* is vital for it expresses the integrating heart of the spirituality. It is represented by the straight line in the centre of the shaded area.

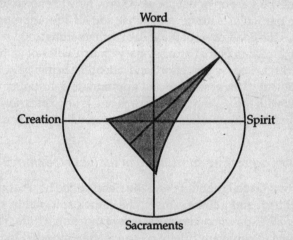

Figure eleven: the enriched core of a maturing spirituality.

In this connection, it is worth noting that many 'spiritualities' are described in a single word; such as 'Ignatian', 'Catholic', 'Pentecostal', 'Evangelical', 'Eucharistic', 'Celtic' and 'creation' spiritualities, to name just a few. The fact that they can be defined in a single word points to the essential core of their nature which holds the whole together.

However, just having a core creates a 'thin' or narrow spirituality, which is why it needs to be *enriched*. The enrichment is expressed in the diagram by the fan; it expands to draw in resources for all four segments of the compass, whilst the core holds them together in an overarching framework. It is this work that constitutes the instructive adventure of the first stage of development of the emerging church.

The outcome of this first, and vital stage, in the development of an emerging missionary orientation of the church, is not simply a verbal statement of the church's beliefs. Rather it will be a lifestyle in which the core values and spiritual vital of the church is expressed. It will be a lived (hence, 'earthed') spirituality – the church being, not just telling, the answers it is discovering. The result will be a group of people who know how to encounter God in their particular setting, and what sort of life appropriately expresses the good news of the gospel in that setting.

What is certain is that a missionary church will not come into being without conscious effort and attention being paid to the development of an accessible and appropriate spirituality which connects with the setting of the church and is an expression of the Christian faith's application to the issues faced by that community.

Stage two: expressing spirituality in the life of the church

The second stage is about taking the riches at the heart of the life of the church and allowing them, the church spirituality, to find appropriate expression in every aspect of the church's life. There is only space to comment briefly on some often repeated issues on the three aspects of *worship*, *community* and *mission*. However, it is sufficient to give ideas about how to proceed in the great variety of churches that make up the Church today.

Worship
In our often frantic, and materially orientated culture, the sense of the transcendent nature of God is particularly needed in worship. In many churches the movement seems to be the other way – towards greater informality and casualness. Yet there is much which suggests

that our culture is hungry for the transcendence, for what lies beyond the mundane. A Catholic priest, when asked why he had incense in his church replied, 'Because you cannot buy it in Marks and Spencer's!' It was a good reply. People come to church because of what they cannot get elsewhere. Yet too easily the Church tries to make itself as much like Marks and Spencer's as it knows how. This is not an argument for outmoded and irrelevant rituals, but it is an argument for seeking to encounter the Otherness of God in worship. There is a hunger for that abroad today, which is why worship, spirituality and mission overlap so much. This is why a vital question each local church needs to address is . . . 'how can we have the kind of worship that may expose others to an experience of God?'[6]

At a recent conference Elisabeth Templeton, a Church of Scotland theologian, made the perceptive comment that 'most people today go to the theatre to be purged and to church to be entertained'. That this is so, is evidence of the failure of nerve and loss of distinctives which has so characterized Western Christianity in the twentieth century. Engagement with life issues, before God, is a vital ingredient in worship.

Lamentation has its part to play here too, for it is an important way in which the Church addresses the brokenness of human society – before God. Equally listening has an important place in worship, for if it has been found that listening is a vital ingredient in the church's spirituality, then a significant place needs to be found for it in the church's worship. It may be that one minute's silence is observed after every reading of Scripture before the response ('This is the word of the Lord . . .') is used. There are good grounds for having the response *after* the silence since there is a double inspiration of Scripture; it is found both in the inspiration of the writers and of the listeners in every age.

Community

The inherited mode of operation of the Church, particularly in its Anglican expression, has not been marked by any great sense of

[6] John Drane, *Evangelism for a New Age*, (Marshall Pickering, 1994) p.120.

community. Indeed the idea of 'making my communion' implies a long-standing individualism and a supermarket (or, filling-station) approach to church membership long before consumerism became a dominant characteristic of our culture. Which is why the introduction of the 'Peace' in communion services has often been felt to be so foreign and intrusive.

It may well have been that in the past inherited mode of being church that other structures of community, both family, extended family and local community, were sufficiently strong for the community aspect of the life of the church to be downplayed. Whatever was the case, it certainly is not that now. Distance and dislocation have broken up the extended family, marriage break-downs have increasingly broken up the nuclear family and local community is in danger of extinction. Caught between the vast and often impersonal structures of national agencies, and multinational corporations, the isolated individual is in a vulnerable position. It is here that the church has a vital role to play: being community where natural community has disappeared. It may well be that the popularity of such soap operas as Coronation Street, Neighbours and the like, express the longing for a form of 'natural community' that is conspicuous by its absence in the real Ramsey and Coronation Streets today.

All too often, however, the church handles relationships like the rest of society. Indeed, it can be argued that the church handles relationships in some ways worse than others:

> One form of love-destroying dishonesty characteristic of life together in our marriages and churches is our niceness. In our niceness we believe that being supportive means never speaking our real thoughts and feelings in areas of disagreement.[7]

> Politeness is the poison of all good collaboration.[8]

---

[7] Roberta Bondi, *To Pray and to Love*, p.107.
[8] Francis Crick, Nobel Prize Winner, quoted by M. Fullan, in *Change forces: probing the depths of educational reform*, p.82.

The lack of a caring community that incarnates the Word makes us more and more incapable of being heard.[9]

Yet there is a desire for community, for belonging. The Christian sees this stemming from our being made in the image of a Trinitarian God. There should be ways in which, despite the limitations of our humanity, that 'living together in love' can become reality. Simply the step of considering how relationships are handled in any particular church, and the commitment to allow the radical message of the Sermon on the Mount to shape the way relationships are handled, would lead to a new openness, acceptance, understanding and ability both to handle conflict and to forgive.

Small (home) groups may well have an important role in the establishing of life-giving, honest and enjoyable relationships. However, we need to notice that fellowship (Greek = *koinonia*) in the New Testament is rarely something that is complete in and of itself. Almost invariably it is 'fellowship in...something'. Indeed the very first use of the word comes in the gospel where we are told that Peter and James had 'koinonia (a partnership) in fishing'. So often in the life of the church, 'fellowship' is seen as an end in itself. When that happens it dies or becomes a complicated way of playing at religion.

. . . groups are very good at developing little rituals of dishonesty, ways of systematically evading real issues.[10]

The real thing comes as often as not when you are doing something together, whether it takes the form of work or play. In terms of the diagram at Figure four on page 86, it is when the three overlapping circles are pulled away from each other and made separate compartments that each aspect suffers. One of the strengths of Base communities is that they have found a way of drawing all three circles together into one gathering/network, energized by their spiritual life.

The emerging church will need to develop the reality of community in its life. This will no doubt happen in a great variety

[9] Melba Maggay, *Transforming Society*, p.21.
[10] Simon Tugwell OP, *Did You Receive the Spirit?* p.122.

of ways. For some it will mean starting home groups, for others a radical reorientating of them around the support of one another to live the whole of life before God. For others it will involve the abandonment of all such structures as new patterns emerge.

For too long the church has heard the call of Jesus Christ to become 'fishers of men' within the notion of the individualism of rod and line. He addressed that call rather to a group who worked with nets. The net the church uses is a network of loving relationships laid down in every network in which its members engage.

Mission

Three distinct areas can be identified where the underlying spirituality of a church should be expressed as far as the mission structures of the church are concerned.

First, attention needs to be paid to *existing structures*. What happens all too often is that the mission structures are in place. Good bridges have been built into the community. Yet, little faith ever crosses that bridge and few unchurched people make the journey to faith across the carefully constructed bridges. The problem is that the bridges have become disconnected from spirituality at the Church end.

So, for example, a church playgroup may well function without any apparent, or actual connection with the Christian faith. An observer coming from outside might well commend such a church for having all the activities in place such as mother-and-toddler groups, playgroups, Sunday schools and uniformed organizations, without noticing that *nothing is getting across* – because nothing is getting out. It is at just such a point that the spiritual dimension needs to be reestablished. For example, playgroup leaders meeting to pray for the work of the group, and to pray for mothers, fathers and families facing difficult situations could transform the environment. Prayer has a way of alerting us to those who are struggling and to words and actions that will touch them with grace, hope and practical help.[11] In prayer we can

[11] Isaiah 50:4-5

discern the leading of the Spirit to reach out in friendship and practical help. Reconnecting such structures is of first importance for a church renewed in its mission focus.

Second, attention needs to be paid to *emerging structures*. Some of the traditional mission structures of the church are looking as if they may have reached their sell-by date. Once marvellous structures for mission, they are now about as relevant to today's work as the 'mercy seat' is to worship. A whole new generation of mission structures is emerging. A number are community action projects seeking to deal with specific problems. Thrift shops, with an associated coffee bar, are meeting needs for cheap clothing and toys as well as for friendship and company. A number of churches are finding such places, *and the quality of uncrowding welcome* experienced, a significant doorway into believing and belonging. Parenting courses are another recent development. Thousands of such groups have been run by churches around the country. These emerging new structures, instead of saying 'come *here* to *hear* what we think is important', are run on the principle of 'going *there* to address *their* concerns'. It is in the latter context that issues of faith will inevitably, and naturally, surface.

Third, attention needs to be paid to what can be called *engaging structures*. There are important new mission structures emerging in work places as Christians (often from different churches) meet together to discern how to function Christianly in that setting. Emerging structures are also evident around 'single issue' needs in the community. This is very much the style advocated in *The Isaiah Vision*, and worked out in *Local Theology*. They may well be short-term projects working in a very ad hoc manner. They model a significant new mission structure. The Church needs to be alive to such developments, able to recognise that this is truly 'church', and give those involved the recognition and support they need. The local church needs to be respectful and protective of such people and activities and not expect that the whole of a person's availability for Christian service should be expressed within the organization structures of the local church.

a first priority must be for Christians to be prepared to go out into the various fragments of local society.[12]

Stage three: sustaining the dialogue

The emphasis in Stage two was on allowing the spirituality to be expressed in the whole life of the church. The movement was, rather like a sunburst, an outward, even explosive, movement. This is so often what happens when a church, for whatever reason and from whatever source, experiences some form of renewal. Life is bursting out all over. It is important to allow this to happen. It is sometimes an experience of springtime in the life of a church – though spring involves hard frosts and the painful breaking open of shells to let out the life of the seed.

However, there is a maturing stage that needs to be gone through. This involves the sustaining of a *continual dialogue between the church and the community*. This also involves a dialogue between life and the tradition of the church. Preaching is one particular way in which this dialogue between life and Scripture is expressed. Indeed I often wonder whether God desires, at the end of each sermon, to be able to hold up the life of the preacher and the community of faith of which he or she is a part, and say – in true Blue Peter style – 'and here is one I prepared earlier!'.

It is this continual dialogue between a changing culture and a church growing (in maturity), that sustains the life of a church. It involves the creative tension of pressing on to discover how the coming of the kingdom is to shape today's situation. One of the key marks of the emerging church is its sense of being on a journey – rather than having arrived. The journey is both defined by the destination – hence the importance of hope, resurrection, kingdom and the End – as 'guiding stars' on this pilgrimage, and energized by the continual dialogue between the tradition/spirituality of the church and the culture/questions of the surrounding communities.

[12] John Reader, *Local Theology*, p.63.

Further reflections

Several principles are likely to prove of great importance in making the shift from inherited to emerging mode.

First, *simplicity* is crucial. Shedding what is no longer needed and simplifying all that is essential are vital in any new development. Cautious holding on to what has been will frustrate the emerging of what will be.

Second, *flexibility* will need to be embraced, as a way of life. It is the antithesis of bureaucracy and institutionalism:

> . . . many new social movements are deliberately loose in their organization, perhaps having no official membership or records. This both makes them harder to pin down and keep under surveillance, and prevents power structures building up within the group . . . it is not the *modus operandi* of most churches.[13]

Third, *purpose* is central. A key distinction between the inherited and emerging modes is that the former sees structures as sacred, whilst the latter sees purpose as sacred and structures as servants. All the time the church needs to come back to the question: 'What is the purpose of this activity/structure/way of doing things?' It then needs to ask the supplementary question, 'Is this still the best or only way of achieving this goal?'

Fourth, *learning* is a key characteristic. Much has been written recently on organisations as potentially 'learning organisations'.[14] The Revd Martin Seeley, responsible for the national network of Continuing Ministerial Training officers, said in a recent lecture on the subject:

> In a learning organisation, however, responsibility and authority is decentralised, and individual responsibility encouraged. Role boundaries are permeable, the system is

---

[13] John Reader, *Local Theology*, p.141.
[14] See, for example, J. Swieringa & A. Wierdsma, *Becoming a Learning Organisation*, and P. Senge, *The Fifth Discipline: the art and practice of the learning organisation*.

open to the wider environment and all elements of the system are open to each other.

Many of the marks of the learning organisation he identifies link with what has already been said about the nature of the emerging church.

Fifth, is the principle of *releasing constraints*.[15] It is easier, when seeking to bring about change, to get hold of the people and factors working for change, and strengthen them. There is a place for doing that. However, often of more importance is identifying the factors and people which are acting as brakes and constraints, finding out why they do, and discovering ways of releasing those constraints. When that happens the forces working for change will come into their own because they are no longer held back.

In all these ways the church can apply its theology and express its spirituality not only through the way that it conducts worship, handles the relationships of the community of faith, and engages with the various worlds inhabited by its members, but by the very way that it seeks to bring about the shift from inherited to emerging mode of being church today. This is the crucial way in which God's people today are to move *forward in faith*.

---

[15] See p.112-115 in my book, *On the anvil*.

11

Reform

The old institutional models are inhibiting new life.
John Reader, *Local Theology*, p.142.

This sickness is not unto death, even though it may be
that only a resurrection can cure it.
John Hull, *What Prevents Christian Adults from
Learning*, p.xi.

It is one thing to have some understanding of what changes need
to be brought about to enable the church to be renewed in mission,
it is another matter to know where and how to begin. It is for this
reason that this chapter addresses the question of where changes
should be looked and worked for. Where should we look to imple-
ment *reform* in such a way as to bring about a shift from the inherited to the emerging mode of being church?

However, before considering specific options, it is important to
address a major preliminary issue. That issue concerns the nature
of the changes we should be looking for. Are we to look for revolution and a whole new beginning, or should we be working for
evolutionary change? Is it 'in for a penny, in for a pound' or
'slowly, slowly catchee monkey'? In other words, should we
abandon the whole inherited mode as outdated or should we seek
to bring about its renewal? Should we, for example, scrap the
parish structure or renew it? This matter clearly needs to be
addressed before we can go any further.

Revolution or evolution?

It is necessary here to introduce the concept of paradigm shifts. A paradigm shift is a whole new way of seeing things. A classic example of a paradigm shift is the revolution in scientific understanding which was brought about by the discovery by Copernicus that the earth rotates around the sun, not the other way. It had, and continues to have, a profound effect on everything we see and do. Paul's Damascus road experience brought about a paradigm shift; a whole new way of seeing life.[1]

In an important work on how scientific changes are brought about, Thomas Kuhn[2] developed the concept of paradigm shift. He argues from the history of the development of scientific ideas that scientific thinking does not follow an easy, natural, evolutionary process. Rather, he says, it proceeds by way of a continual breakdown of one way of seeing things which provokes a whole new way of understanding. Thus, Einstein, sensing the limitations of Newtonian physics, looked for a whole new framework in which to view physics. It led him to develop the theory of relativity.

This principle of paradigm shifts has been applied to many other disciplines, including that of both the history of Christian theology as a whole[3] and the history of the theology of mission.[4] Applying this idea of the need for paradigm shifts to the subject of this book would point us in the direction of radical new beginnings. We live, it has been argued, in such a changed cultural context that we need to find 'new ways of being church'. What is more, when we start looking, we do find groups of people seeking to develop whole new ways of expressing the life of the church. Base communities are one such contemporary manifestation in this 'creative discontinuity' with the established Church. Certainly, individuals and groups need to be given the freedom,

[1] Philippians 3 spells out the radical changes that resulted for Paul.
[2] Thomas Kuhn, *The Structure of Scientific Revolutions*.
[3] Hans Kung, *Paradigm Change in Theology*.
[4] David Bosch, *Transforming Mission*.

space, authority and resources to develop new ways of expressing the life of the church.

However, there is a counterargument which challenges the whole thesis of paradigm shift as developed by Thomas Kuhn. Change, it is argued, is the result not of one massive step but rather of a series of many, largely imperceptible, steps on an evolutionary path. One seemingly different perspective is actually the fruit of taking the last idea further forward. Apart from Base communities, all the models identified in Chapter five actually fit this approach. They involve the reworking of existing models of church.

My observation of churches is that models of both ways of making the shift to a missionary orientation are already emerging. There are whole new beginnings taking place. There are also striking ways in which the inherited model is being reworked around a mission orientation. What we need to look out for, therefore, are signs of both revolutionary new beginnings and evolutionary changes to the existing patterns of being church.

In doing so it is important for us to be aware of the relationship between these two forms of church life. That relationship is the same as the one between tugs and a liner in their joint role of getting people by sea from one country to another. Tugs are small and powerful boats which are necessary to get the liner out of the harbour without its grounding on the sandbanks. They give the liner direction. However, you would need a vast number of tugs to transport two thousand people across the Atlantic – and it would certainly not be in the comfort they could expect on a liner. The tugs are, in that sense, secondary to the liner, for it is the liner that will transport the people across the ocean. Yet, without the tugs, they would not only not be able to make their journey; they might well lose their lives in the venture.

So, in the development of emerging patterns of church life, we need radical new developments. Without them the liner of the church will not be able to get out to sea. However, we also need to develop the liner in such a way that it can carry the people across that sea. So we need both the new developments *and* the reworking of the existing model.

With this view of what we need to look for, we turn now to specific ways in which the emergence of new patterns of church life can be seen and can be encouraged. The options are set out within a threefold framework. First, we will consider the revolutionary way – the development of new ways of being church. Then we will look at the evolutionary way, and about how different aspects of the existing church can be renewed in mission. Finally, we will consider how an inner revolution of how the church functions can be evolved within the outward framework of the inherited mode. This latter approach I have called the dispersed model.

First option: new ways of being church

In the midst of the radical changes taking place in our culture today it is important that groups of people are given the freedom to find new patterns for church life. The Late Late Service in Glasgow, the Joy Service in Oxford and the Nine O'Clock Service in Sheffield[5] are three such 'new ways of being church' related particularly to the youth culture. They have all emerged out of an attempt by the church to engage with that culture,[6] though their relevance extends well beyond that specific age group and culture.

Other new ways of being church include the use of the Base community as a model, and the focusing of the life of the church around its missionary calling. The latter is being expressed by such developments as church-in-the-community projects, established by the Church's Urban Fund. Church planting is another way in which groups can be given the freedom to develop new models of being church. However, there are dangers with such an approach as far as the renewal in mission is concerned. First, they can all too easily simply reject the riches and insight of the church and focus entirely on being up-to-date and relevant. There is much that is good in that instinct, but those who reject the lessons of history usually end up repeating the mistakes of the past. When

[5] See Chapter 12 (Nine O'Clock in the Evening) of my book *In the Crucible* for the story and thinking behind its development.
[6] Ibid.

such 'new churches' fail to take on their journey the riches of the church's insights they too easily become modernist churches in a post-modern culture.

There is a place for some church plants being 'more of the same' in the sense of the evolutionary development to which we will shortly turn. However, they are a glorious opportunity to draw on the riches of the past and yet give them fresh interpretation and expression. It is to be hoped that we will, in due course, see models of this type of church planting in which the implications of the previous chapter are being worked out. They could serve a vital role in the church of the future.

A further important option for developing new ways of being church is in the creation of new congregations. One of the particular advantages of this approach is that it enables a church to develop 'new ways of being church' from within the existing structures. Moreover, it is often less disruptive. So, for example, a church of forty to fifty members with an average age of around fifty is really very unlikely to be able to make the changes that will enable its worship to become the natural place for young people in their late teens and early twenties to feel at home. There needs to be a new beginning. Such a church might well be best advised to keep the existing congregation going whilst developing another whole new way of congregation for a different group at a different time. It was this that was the basis of the development of the Nine O'Clock Service in which I was involved in my last parish. It is all part of the learning to speak the two languages of the 'old order' and the 'new order' in the period of transition which society is going through at present. Some churches are experimenting with congregations meeting on days other than Sunday.

Second option: renewing existing ways of being church

The question remains for most churches as to how they might bring about the reorientating of the church which this book has called for. Here it will be helpful to suggest a number of practical possibilities.

First, the *home group*, or any small 'primary' (that means 'face-to-face') group set up specifically for this purpose. Here is an opportunity for people with a vision and heart for what has been addressed to be allowed to explore the implications for themselves. Some minimum necessary relating to the church should be spelt out – rather along the lines of Acts 15 where a minimalist list was drawn up. What is needed is the giving of permission and encouragement. Those involved in such a grouping will need to keep in good contact with the leadership of the church, both to receive help and guidance but also as a way of informing, and probably educating, the church's leadership.

Second, *work groups*, in which people working in the same areas of employment (e.g. teachers or shop-floor workers) can come together and seek to relate their faith to their working environment. Many smaller churches will not have enough people to make this viable. However, there is an even better way of operating which they can attempt to develop. This is to encourage church members to form groups within particular settings, such as a local hospital where members of other churches also work. I know of one hospital where a new-style 'Christian Union' gathers together church members working in any role in the hospital. Consultants and porters, administrators and cleaners come together to affirm their faith and address the issues which confront them in this environment. I describe this as a new-style 'Christian Union' since the old style of such a grouping usually only addresses 'spiritual' and 'evangelism' issues. New-style groupings will address, rather, the moral issues and the matter of confronting the principalities and powers within the working structure. They will be whole-life-focused, not 'religious-life-focused' groups.

Third, *congregations*. As part of the diversity and fragmentation of life today many churches are experiencing the fact that different congregations have a character and feel of their own. What is different now is that this is being acknowledged and encouraged, rather than resisted. When it happens it does present the church with a challenge to find ways of holding the whole church together; but that can be achieved. What is said above about congregations, under the first option, applies equally here at this point.

Fourth, church life *process*. The last chapter identified a flow of reflection along the line of world-spirituality-worship-community-mission. It was pointed out there that although the first step of developing a dialogue between the setting of the church ('world') and its spirituality, seemed to be the natural starting point; application could then deal with *worship, community* and *mission* in any order that seemed appropriate. What was being proposed was a long-term process of reflection on experience and subsequent action. Indeed it may well be wise and right for a church to think in terms of a five-year plan for such a process, in which study groups to reflect on the issues, experimentation, sermon series and prayer-focus all have their part to play.

Fifth, *aspects* of the life of the church can also be dealt with a step at a time. It may be that the home groups or the work of the PCC, the youth group or the preaching are the right place to begin working on bringing about the shifts identified in this book. What may well happen is that lessons will be learned which will avoid inflicting the same mistakes on the whole church and will make change in other areas a speedier work. It may well be that when ways of working are developed which relate more naturally to the setting of the whole church that other groups in the church will be saying, in effect, 'Why can't we work that way?'.

Third option: dispersed ways of being church

The primary weakness of the parish system, as currently understood and practised, is that it is built on the assumption that people live and work within a specific geographical area. That has been true in the past and is illustrated in the diagram below (Figure twelve). The concentric circles indicate that each 'world' contains the other 'world' but goes beyond it. The diagonal lines express the fact that in such a setting the underlying worldview of the church and wider society are the same. This is the

Christendom framework in which the church has existed for most of its time in the United Kingdom. Evangelism in such a context is done by awakening the latent faith in the fringe members of the church. The culture has ensured that, like flowers in the desert, the faith has already been planted. All that is needed is for the plants to be watered.

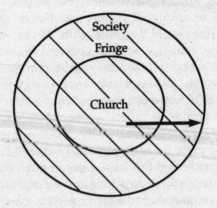

Figure twelve: Christendom – geographical view of parish and evangelism.

Our problem today is that this geographical way of relating, and the underlying acceptance of a Christian worldview, are fast disappearing and in many places have already completely gone. Even from the perspective of rural ministry in Shropshire, John Reader says:

> Perhaps in the old days, when local society was a mono-chrome and hierarchical structure, there was a coherent community and the Church of England could claim to be at the heart of it, but only because it was identified with the upper echelons of the structure. Now that this pattern of social relationships has been broken, the only option seems to be to live within the fragments.[7]

[7] John Reader, *Local Theology*, p.53.

Today well under half of the population establish relationships on the basis of geographical proximity to others. People in the UK today relate sociologically more than geographically. They relate to those with whom they perceive themselves to have something in common more than to those they live next to.

Moreover, in the mobile culture in which we live, much living is done in a whole series of different worlds – the worlds of work, leisure and shopping may well be dozens of miles from a person's home. It is often only children, mothers who work full time at caring for them and running the home, and the elderly who feel any sense of being part of 'the local community', though the unemployed sometimes come into this grouping as well. *A church model based exclusively on where people live is likely to be irrelevant to many unless it finds new ways of operating*. The implications for the parish system are immense, the more so when one enters the major conurbations in which many people live and work.

The present situation is expressed in Figure thirteen. The Christendom worldview is inhabited by a minority of the population. There are many other, competing perspectives. These include not only other faith-communities, but the secular, materialistic teleculture which most people inhabit. Moreover, the various different shapes in this diagram can also be seen as expressing the fact that most people actually 'inhabit' several different worlds. The worlds of work, home, leisure, church and politics are often very separate worlds.

> The process of secularization has resulted in an amazing variety of independent worlds. Many people today live in a variety of worlds such as family, job, leisure, politics and education. These worlds represent different social structures.[8]

We meet different people there, we do different things, we approach life from a different perspective, we talk a different language. Evangelism in such a setting involves entering into the

[8] *The Church for Others* (WCC Report) p.83.

varied worldviews and perspectives of these different groups (the dotted lines), learning to speak their language and express the Christian faith from within the setting (the continuous lines). That articulation of the faith from within each culture is likely to result in a variety of ways of being church that appropriately express that faith.

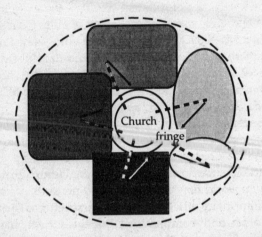

Figure thirteen: contemporary sociological patterns of relating and mission.

As the *Local Theology* model shows, the existing inherited model of church can be reshaped to function in this dispersed way, engaging the issues and networks around the church. It was clearly not without difficulty, but, whilst retaining the outward form of the church, a profound refocusing of the life of a typical parish church was possible.

It is worth noting in this connection that one of the major trends in the way that the church is operating today may well be helpful to the development of a dispersed model of church life. I refer to what are now called 'multibenefice parishes'. These are parishes where one vicar has a considerable number of churches for which he is responsible, sometimes into double figures. This is happening not least as a result of the reduction in the number of clergy and churchgoers. However, rather than, for example, close six village churches and get all the worshippers into one central place, the church has to operate differently. This is both because not everyone has transport, but also because people feel they belong to the village but not to the nearest market town where a 'big church' might be kept open. Rightly the trend is towards keeping all the 'outlets' open.

This brings two major advantages. First, the clergy simply cannot 'do it all'. Their role changes from doing all the ministry to equipping church members for that work.[9] This is having the effect of a considerable liberation of the whole church into the work that rightly belonged to it in the first place – before hierarchical structures robbed the laity of their ministry. Second, these large groupings do create the space for some of the non-parochial structures we have discussed in this chapter to have space to emerge. In this larger group it is possible to develop alternative ways of worship (such as youth worship, and the like) and grouping for mission (such as Christians working in local schools or places of employment). This process of pastoral reorganization may well be a helpful framework within which a dispersed model of church life can emerge.

Conclusion

Whichever of the above three ways proves most appropriate in any particular situation, it needs to be said that if new ways of being church are to emerge they will require something more radical than new structures. The Romans, those supreme organizers, learned this many years ago:

> We trained hard but it seems that every time we were beginning to form into teams we would be re-organized. I was to learn, later in life, that we tend to meet any new situation by re-organizing, and a wonderful method it can be for creating

[9] See Ephesians 4:12.

the illusion of progress whilst producing confusion, ineffi-
ciency and demoralization.[10]

The shift from inherited to emerging modes of church life will
necessitate new ways of being church members and new ways of
being clergy. New church structures necessitate new church
people. To that final aspect of the development of the church
renewed in mission we turn next.

---

[10] Petronius Arbiter (A.D. 66), quoted in *Surviving in Teams*, p.10.

12

Priesthood for Change

The needs of the world, not the concerns of the church,
are primary to an understanding of effective evangelism.

John Drane, *Evangelism for a New Age*, p.75.

Mankind was created priest of the world, the one who
offers the world to God in a sacrifice of love and praise
and who, through the external eucharist, bestows the
divine love upon the world.

Alexander Schmemann, *The world as sacrament* p.114.

It is people who bring about change. For that to happen they need
to be changed people, or rather, changing people, for conversion is
a way of life not a moment's experience. But the change to which
the gospel points us is one which, whilst transforming the individual, embraces God's purpose for the whole of creation. We are
called to be new creatures, not least by our participation in his
making all things new – even a new heaven and a new earth.[1]
There can be no retreat into a purely individual interpretation of
faith or of evangelism. The mission of God, like the robe of Christ,
is seamless.

In view of the vastness of the scope of God's purposes and the
testing circumstances in which we find ourselves today, our
response must surely be the same as Peter's when he contem-
plated the ultimate purposes of God, namely, 'What kind of people

[1] 2 Corinthians 5:17 with Revelation 21:5 and Revelation 21:1.

ought you to be?'[2] The answer to his question which I want to highlight in this chapter is the answer that Peter himself gave in his first Epistle, by drawing attention to the priestly nature of the Church:

> But you are a chosen people, a royal priesthood, a holy nation, a people belonging to God, that you may declare the praises of him who called you out of darkness into his wonderful light.[3]

It is in the renewal of our understanding and practice of priesthood that we are most likely to find the resources we need to be part of the emerging church renewed in mission. We will consider the implications of the renewal of the priesthood of the church from four different aspects.

A missionary priesthood

We begin by considering the role of the ordained ministry in the emerging church. Clearly, a missionary church will need a missionary priesthood; leaders able to equip the church for its mission of being fully human and participating in the humanizing work of the kingdom of God. That will involve a major shift of priorities and of style for clergy. The emerging church requires a very different approach to 'the ministry' from the church in inherited mode. Not only that, but a church seeking to make a shift from inherited to emerging mode needs a leadership able to manage change.

This presents a major challenge to clergy at a time when their task of sustaining the inherited mode of being church seems to be an increasingly difficult, and for some, discouraging task. It is important not to underestimate those pressures. However, to use a farming illustration, although it is not easy to shift from using a spade to using a tractor, in the long run it certainly makes the job easier. However, the setting is not easy, as the following story illustrates.

[2] 2 Peter 3:11.
[3] 1 Peter 2:9.

In the latter stages of this book I had the opportunity to talk with a senior Anglican Bishop about the subject and was using the illustration of 'the tugs and liner' to explain how I saw that changes might come about. Our conversation, however, took place within a couple of weeks of the disastrous journey of the QE2 across the Atlantic with plumbers still working on the refit. We began to play around with that experience of the QE2 as a metaphor of the church's experience. We saw how like the life of the church it was, for the task of refitting the church for the next stage of its journey has to take place whilst on the voyage. We do not have the luxury of closing the church for a year and starting up in a new way of working at the end of the year. As indicated earlier, clergy need to be 'bilingual' able to work in two different cultures. It is a testing task. We also recognized that the task of the church is made more difficult by the fact that many on board as plumbers actually function as if they were passengers. We concluded that, difficult though the task is, the refit must go ahead and that the long-term benefits will be there for all to enjoy.

Certainly there are some clergy who sense that so much is changing around them that they are not sure whether there is a job for them. Does, for example, collaborative ministry make leadership redundant? Or does seeing the church functioning in dispersed mode 'out in the world' make clergy very much laymen and laywomen when it comes to equiping people to function Christianly in the health service, or the worlds of education, business, self-employment or bioethics?

My conviction is that there is a vital role for ordained leadership within the church, but it is a *changed* role. Those changes have to be made if that new role is to be discovered. In many places they are already being made. Three marks of such a 'new order of ministry' are identified in what follows. It should be noted that they are put in terms of 'A rather than B', indicating a spectrum. It does not mean that 'B' must now be abandoned, but rather that 'A' needs to be the new norm, with 'B' taking a secondary place.

Long term this has major implications for the selection, training and deployment of clergy. For the present we will see how it might affect the way the work of the ministry is being conducted today.

First, the church stands in need of leadership modelled on the role of *conductor* rather than *director*. The director is essentially an imperial, hierarchical approach to leadership. It is not an efficient way of working. The conductor (of an orchestra, not a bus!) is a more appropriate model. The conductor does, of course, do plenty of 'direction', but it is geared to the releasing and harmonizing of the gifts of others. In fact, the conductor is the one person in the orchestra who does not play an instrument. As has already been pointed out, both the shortage of clergy and the vitality of the laity mean that the only way forward for the church will be by the releasing of gifts, energies and skills of the whole people of God. It is in and through them that the vision for this particular church may well emerge, rather than through the ordained minister. It is certainly only through 'the whole people of God' that any vision can be implemented.

The business world has recognized this principle in identifying the importance of 'steering rather than rowing'.[4] Rowing is about doing all the work. Steering is about making the strategic, shaping contribution to the work of others.

Too often, the feudal past has handed down a pattern of leadership modelled more on the role of the orchestra than that of the conductor. In that situation the priest is the one who plays all the instruments. Letting go of the desire, and need, to be in control of everything, know everything and do everything, is fundamental to the emerging of a new way of being priests. Difficult new skill though it is, it can be enormously liberating.

In speaking about priests as conductors I have several times been challenged by those who, taking up the musical analogy, have argued that the church should be playing jazz, which is entirely a matter of improvising rather than working to a fixed script. There is much to be said for this approach, and the idea has been explored in full in at least one book. As the author of that book puts it:

[4] Spelt out in Tom Peters, *In Search of Excellence*.

> People who think they have created an indestructible vision simply issue a command, write an agenda. Had Odysseus sailed home according to an agenda, the account of his voyage would not be worth remembering.[5]

Those who feel they need to be working to a script (Scripture) must remember that no conductor (leader) or orchestra (church) has ever handled the script of the gospel without their own interpretation being expressed in it. Indeed, that is the reason for *their* playing it. It is those who think they are simply handling 'objective truth' who most easily fool themselves – though not many others.

Second, the church today needs leaders who function more as *facilitators* rather than *providers*. There is an important distinction between doing things *for* people, doing things *with* people and enabling people to do things for *themselves*. Certainly the inherited pattern has been one of 'providing services'. It has many subtle pressures and dysfunctional aspects. It tends to be built around a person in leadership with an unrecognized, and so unresolved, need either to achieve or to be needed. When that happens the church is alternately exhaustingly active or soporifically passive. Neither mode works the works of God. Rather, in the likeness of Jesus, the church needs leadership which is continually saying 'You can do it.' It is this confidence placed in people which will draw out latent skills, energy and commitment. Leadership needs to function primarily in permission-giving rather than permission-withholding mode. Fear of failure, and of others failing, needs to be addressed here.

> A critical skill we need to teach ourselves and our people is how to fail – how to learn our lessons from the experience of defeat and pick ourselves up again and start anew.[6]

This also involves the development of a collaborative style of ministry. This represents a shift from the soloist role into the team-player role. It is rooted in the understanding of the Trinity, not least

---

[5] Max De Pree, *Leadership Jazz*, p.40. See also his *Leadership is an Art*.
[6] Melba Maggay, *Transforming Society*, p.93.

as community-in-mission.[7] At this point deep-seated instincts in clergy and churches may need to be brought to the surface, faced and resolved. These instincts arise from centuries of accumulated expectation about the role of the clergy in the life of the church. Some of those expectations are false, unhealthy and now inappropriate. They have to be confronted. Difficult though this is, the fruit of doing so is liberating. 'The ministry' is essentially what the whole church, not just the person, does. When we recognize this then impossible expectations can be avoided.

Third, and perhaps more controversially, the church today needs clergy functioning more as *leaders* than *managers*. There are some important objections to this idea.

An objection from clergy is that they were ordained to be pastors, not managers or leaders. Certainly pastoral care is the primary work of clergy in the inherited mode. However, the move into collaborative styles of ministry means that clergy need to think and act more in terms of 'ensuring that everyone is cared for' rather than the impossible task of 'caring for everyone'. Again there is liberation built into this shift – freeing clergy from unrealistic expectations and from the unhealthy provider/client role.

A further objection to making a shift from managers to leaders is expressed by those involved in clergy support and in-service training who say, 'We have only just begun to get clergy to see the need for proper management of the church; are you now going to undo that hard-won progress?'. There is important truth in that objection. No operation, particularly in our market culture, can survive without proper management. Certainly churches need to be well managed, and clergy need to learn those skills, but – and this is my point – without the leadership dimension the church will simply be an organization, not a community-in-mission.

Another objection comes from those who fear that the emphasis on leadership will be taken as a lapse back into 'one-man ministry' and undo the painstakingly slow work of establishing a

[7] This whole principle is worked out with great thoroughness in Robin Greenwood's important new contribution to a contemporary understanding of the ministry, *Transforming Priesthood*.

collaborative style of leadership. My answer here is that leadership needs to be seen as a servant role in the sense of this being a necessary contribution to any operation. But leadership is needed. Often it is the articulation of a shared vision, sometimes it is the authentication of a vision that emerges from someone other than the leader. As John Reader puts it:

> If Christian leadership involves vision, I would want to translate this as meaning seeing the possibilities in a particular situation.[8]

The fact is any operation needs leadership to function fully. The business world is particularly aware at present of the fact that it tends to have *too many managers and too few leaders*. Certainly the leadership I am advocating is a teamworking, facilitating, enabling style, but it is nonetheless leadership for being that. Churches whose life is most healthy and alive, are almost invariably churches which have worked out how to encourage and support clear and creative leadership and active participation in discerning and implementing the vision owned by all. Clear leadership and good collaborative styles are great when properly harnessed together. Apart they are unbalanced and often result in loss of vitality.

Fourth, the church today needs its leadership to see itself as *persons* rather than *parsons*. If the gospel is about being human, then the leadership within the church must model what that means.

> The greatest saints of God have been characterized, not by haloes and an atmosphere of distant unapproachability, but by their humanity.[9]

Being parsons is about being in a role whilst being persons is about being whole. Seeing ourselves as people first is vital to our own health as well as the health of the church. Essential to that is the

[8] John Reader, *Local Theology*, p.74.
[9] James Philip, *Christian Maturity*, p.70.

capacity not to take ourselves too seriously. In the work of God in which clergy are involved there is an occupational hazard of missing the distinction between taking God seriously and taking ourselves seriously. It was Emperor Hirohito of Japan, the last divinized ruler of Japan, who said, 'You cannot imagine the extra work I had when I was a god.'. The church needs clergy who can laugh at themselves, not take their work too seriously. After all, in the final issue, it is *God's* work.

The changes I have suggested as needed in the way that clergy do their work are major ones. However, as has been pointed out at each turn, it is important to grasp that the fruit of such changes is likely to be a more relaxed and realistic definition of what one person can contribute to a team of from dozens to hundreds of people. In the end, this should be good news to church and clergy alike, and a major motivation for working through the cost of such shifts.

A priestly people

The emerging missionary church needs not only a missionary priesthood, but a missionary people. By this is meant church members who see themselves as called to participate in God's mission in the whole of their living. This has been the whole-life focus of the emerging church to which this book has been pointing.

> The Body which makes the Word visible is not limited to the local church. The *ecclesia visibilis* is God's people making the presence of the kingdom felt in all areas of life, the leaven which permeates all of human activity. It is the church in academia, the church in politics, the church in the market-place.[10]

The loss of Christian distinctives, by which the church proclaims the gospel through its life style, has had a significant diluting effect

[10] Melba Maggay, *Transforming Society*, p.21.

on the witness of the church. All too often evangelism is simply introducing people to what may be called 'bolt-on spirituality'. By this is meant that people coming to faith are led into some initial encounter with God, but that experience is not properly related to or grounded in the whole life of the person. As a result an experience of God is bolted onto a secular worldview, life style, value system and personal identity. When testing comes, including the moral decisions which go to make up our experience of life, such a person is likely to make response out of the secular worldview in which they still function. Three American writers have expressed this well about the church in America:

> The contemporary American church is so largely enculturated to the American ethos of consumerism that it has little power to believe or act.[11]

> Just as the identity of a modern American is in part defined by the commitment to life, liberty and the pursuit of happiness, so the identity of those who have entered into the Israel of God is defined by a commitment to pursue love for God and the neighbour.[12]

> What people believe no longer makes much difference to how they behave.[13]

Much the same can be said about the Church in the whole of the West, including our country.

One of the ways of addressing this situation is evidenced in the renewal of the catechumenate and in the significant shift to a process approach to evangelism whereby people have time and opportunity to engage in a dialogue with the faith and take it into their whole life style. Ways need to be found of evangelizing the whole person. Establishing the new, and existing, believer in a Christian worldview focused upon the purposes of God is the

---

[11] Walter Brueggemann, *The Prophetic Imagination*, p.11.
[12] William Abraham, *The Logic of Evangelism*, p.35.
[13] Os Guinness in an article on mission modernity in *Transformation* magazine.

pastoral work that needs to be done. It will include establishing people in a Christian identity as one baptized into Christ and his filial relationship with the Father, and called to reflect the divine nature and the values of the age to come in the whole of life. A church, renewed in the quality of its faith and in the secure Christian identity of its members, would find a watching world eager to know more of the source of its joy, faith, courage, justice and love.

As the Archbishops' Commission on Rural Areas affirms, baptism is the basis of the constitution of the church and its mission. Rightly understood, *baptism is the commissioning of the laity into the priestly, prophetic and kingly ministry of Christ.* Indeed, we may need to talk about baptism as the ordination of the laity, the foundational ministry in the church, with priesthood as a secondary and derived ministry emerging out of that foundational one, if we are to break out of the deeply clerical nature of the church in inherited mode. Baptism is the ordination of the laity.[14] which defines and energizes both our identity and our mission.

> Christ revealed the essence of priesthood to be love, and, therefore, priesthood to be the essence of life.[15]

Once this is grasped as the foundational ministry of the church it shifts the perspective of the believer from one of spectator to participator, and from consumer of, to worker in, God's mission to the world.

This is essentially the work of increasing the *quality* of faith and discipleship in existing members of the church, yet its knock-on effect is likely to stimulate the *quantity* of newcomers. It is only this renewal of the Christian identity of all believers, as ordained into Christ's ministry of prophet, priest and king, that will give the members of the church the resources, grace and confidence to function Christianly in their daily lives.

The renewal of the baptismal identity of every Christian could do more for their own holiness, the vitality and distinctiveness of

[14] John 15:16 and Romans 6.
[15] Alexander Schmenann, *The world as sacrament*, p.115

the church, and the transformation of our society into that 'civilization of love' than any other single emphasis in the life of the church today. This is the heart of the real pastoral work that needs to take place within the church. It is not about keeping people happy, but making them holy – and sharing in that mutual process with them. It is where the spirituality which lies at the heart of vital church life is to be found – in the new identity in Christ in which all believers participate.

A priestly community

One of the weaknesses of the Reformation attempt to establish the priesthood of all believers was the unconscious individualism with which they read such phrases as 'a royal priesthood'. They missed the essentially corporate nature of the concept. Yes, there is a sense in which each of the fifty members of the average church has a priestly function. Nonetheless, the primary priestly role each one has is by being part of the one priesthood of the church. The church is the primary agent of mission through its corporate identity as a royal priesthood.

Of the hundreds of texts in the Old Testament about priesthood which the New Testament writers could have drawn on, the writers of 1 Peter and Revelation, drew on just two:

You will be to me a kingdom of priests and a holy nation.

You will be called priests of the Lord, you will be named ministers of our God.[16]

The striking thing about these two texts is that they are virtually the only ones that speak in terms of the whole nation of Israel, rather than the tribe of Levi, as a priesthood. It is this corporate nature of the priesthood of the church which needs to be recovered in the emerging church.

[16] Exodus 19:6 and Isaiah 61:6. For further treatment of this theme, see 'The Priesthood of the Church' in John Robinson's, *On Being the Church in the World*, p.72ff.

One of the ways in which this can already be seen to be taking place is in the research of John Finney on how people come to faith.[17] He established the fact that most people come to faith through friendship with a church member. This certainly includes a one-to-one relationship, but the phrase 'church member' points to an overlooked fact. It is not just the one-to-one relationship but the way that relationship with a church member introduces someone into the faith community in which something of that 'different way of seeing and living life' is evident. In a society where many relationships and community structures are breaking down and leaving people alone before vast, impersonal and bureaucratic governmental and industrial organizations, there is a hunger for relationship. The church as *community* functions as a pilot project for the Age to Come, and as a priestly faith community.

Vital though the baptismal identity of every believer is, it is at least as important that the essentially corporate nature of priest-hood is grasped and lived out. Where people hitherto have looked to the building or the clergy as symbols of 'church', the emerging church will point (because the emerging culture is increasingly looking) to the faith community. The inherited mode of church was largely institutional, hence the focus on buildings and official representatives. The way in which people today, in the emerging culture, are seeking to find community is through the two key aspects of *intimacy* and *networks*.[18] Evangelism is working where *intimacy* leads to an introduction to the church as a *network* of loving relationships, however imperfect those relationships may yet be. It is this that makes the handling of the inner life of the church, particularly its spirituality and sense of community, so important, for the church proclaims the gospel simply by *being* the church. As T.S. Eliot put it:

> There is no life that is not lived in community, and no community not lived in praise of God.[19]

[17] John Finney, *Finding Faith Today*.
[18] See John Reader, *Local Theology*, Chapters 2 and 7.
[19] T.S. Eliot, *Collected Poems 1909-1935*, p.164.

The priestly mission

Having considered the handling of the theme of priesthood in 1 Peter and Revelation, we turn finally to Paul's treatment of the theme:

> I have written to you quite boldly on some points, as if to remind you of the grace God gave me to be a minister of Christ Jesus to the Gentiles with the priestly duty of proclaiming the gospel of God, so that the Gentiles might become an offering acceptable to God, sanctified by the Holy Spirit.[20]

This transposition of priesthood from a cultic, individual and church-life key to an outgoing and evangelistic one is quite striking. It raises the question about how evangelism is likely to be evident in the emerging church. I suggest that the following marks will be evident.

Evangelism in the emerging church will begin with *listening*, and will arise out of it. It will be out of a lived response to the questions which life and culture are asking of all people. This is what the third section of this book, on being human, was seeking to do. Living the gospel response to the answers to contemporary questions is where the church will be heard; not that we should be thinking of, or looking for, totally complete answers. Living with unanswered questions is part of what it means to live Christianly. This listening way of evangelism is strongly evident in the way that Jesus answered each person in a way unique to them. He did not come with a stock set of answers. He listened to the person, and the Spirit, and spoke out of that hearing.[21]

Evangelism in the emerging church will be *integrated* with the whole of life. Evangelism has too easily become detached from life, and even church life. The whole thrust of this book is that as the church lives the gospel as a faith community and participates in God's mission to the whole of creation, it will take on board a

[20] Romans 15:15-16.
[21] Isaiah 50:4-5, John 5:19.

whole-life focus. It will be both engaged yet distinctive:

> . . . the Christian style of life is marked by an extraordinary
> combination of detachment and concern. The Christian will
> care less for the world and at the same time care more for it
> than the person who is not a Christian. He will not lose his
> heart to it, but may well lose his life for it.[22]

Opportunities to speak of one's faith are likely to be greatly
increased because one is engaging with the agenda of the world,
with the issues that concern those among whom we live and
work. Christianity seen primarily as a way of 'doing things differently', rather than, as in the inherited mode, a way of 'doing
different things', means that faith and life are constantly inter-
secting.

Evangelism will be likely to function much more in terms of
telling stories. As the early disciples put it: 'We cannot but speak of
the things we have seen and heard.' Speaking will be from the
experience of encountering God's grace, enjoying the life of the
faith community and finding the courage to hold on in the midst of
difficult and testing circumstances. *The words that people can hear
today are through stories that incarnate the truth, more than through
arguments that prove it.* Not that the work of apologetics is unim-
portant. However, we live in a world which, like Eliza Dolittle is
saying, 'Words, words, words what do they mean? Don't talk at
all, show me.'.

Evangelism in the emerging church will also be marked by
answering. As 1 Peter puts it:

> . . . always be prepared to give an answer to everyone who
> asks you to give a reason for the hope that you have.[23]

Perhaps the most important word in that sentence is 'hope', for
this is one of the key distinctives of the Christian faith, as along
with the rest of humanity, we face the uncertainties of the shifting

---

[22] John Robinson, *On Being the Church in the World*, p.18.
[23] 1 Peter 3:15.

culture in which we live. The kingdom, the resurrection and the promise of the Age to Come, sustain the church as it presses on to participate in God's mission, even when many setbacks are experienced and when others have given up hope.

A vision of a priestly people

We conclude with an account from the earliest days of the Christian Church, which can tell us something of how the emerging church will need to live its life and fulfill its calling. It comes from a letter written in Asia Minor around A.D. 150. It tells us not about the Church in the sense of its organization and way of operating, but about the fruits of faith in the life of its members. It is a wonderful, visionary, picture of the church in mission mode. As such it leaves us with a vision for us as we pray and work for the renewal of the church in mission in our day.

> *For Christians are not distinguished from the rest of mankind by country, or by speech, or by dress. For they do not dwell in cities of their own, or use a different language, or practise a peculiar life. This knowledge of theirs has not been proclaimed by the thought and effort of restless men; they are not champions of a human doctrine, as some men are. But while they dwell in Greek or barbarian cities according as each man's lot has been cast, and follow the customs of the land in clothing and food, and other matters of daily life, yet the condition of citizenship which they exhibit is wonderful, and admittedly strange. They live in countries of their own, but simply as sojourners; they share the life of citizens, they endure the lot of foreigners; every foreign land is to them a fatherland, and every fatherland a foreign land. They marry like the rest of the world, they breed children, but they do not cast their offspring adrift. They have a common table, but yet not common. They exist in the flesh, but they live not after the flesh. They spend their existence upon earth, but their citizenship is in heaven. They obey the established laws, and in their own lives they surpass the laws. They love all men, and are persecuted by all. They*

are unknown, and they are condemned; they are put to death, and they gain new life. They are poor, and make many rich; they lack everything, and in everything they abound. They are dishonoured, and their dishonour becomes their glory; they are reviled, and are justified. They are abused, and they bless; they are insulted, and repay insult with honour. They do good, and are punished as evil-doers; and in their punishment they rejoice as gaining new life therein... In a word, what the soul is in the body Christians are in the world.[24]

God grant that such might be said, of the churches of which we are members, in the years to come.

---

[24] J. Stevenson, *A New Eusebius*, p.58.